Lace TO USE

Lace TO USE

JEAN WITHERS

Dryad Press Ltd
LONDON

Acknowledgment

My thanks must go to many friends and students for their interest
and encouragement, especially June and Stanley Jackson for taking
and preparing the photographs, Helen Jackson for modelling some
of the items illustrated, June Jackson and Margaret Lawrence for
checking the draft manuscript, June Jackson for making the blouse
illustrated in Fig. 102, my husband John for producing the
manuscript on his office word-processor, his business partners Pam
and Garry Payne for allowing him to do so, and last but not least my
son Ian, not only for his assistance in sorting, fetching and carrying,
but also for keeping out of the way when his help was not required!

British Library Cataloguing in Publication Data

Withers, Jean
  Lace to use.
  1. Handicrafts using lace – Manuals
  I. Title
  746.2′2

ISBN 0 85219 738 1

Typeset by Keyspools Ltd, Golborne, Lancs
and printed in Great Britain by
The Bath Press Ltd
Bath
for the publishers
Dryad Press Ltd
8 Cavendish Square
London W1M 0AJ

Contents

Introduction

Many people enjoy the challenge of working fine traditional prickings and mounting them in a traditional way, but then feel that their lace is too precious to use. It is, however, satisfying to be able to make use of the results of your efforts, and this book sets out to stimulate ideas for using lace in ways both suited to today's pace of life and easy to care for.

Various patterns and prickings for clothing, accessories and household use have been included. All the prickings (which include Torchon, Beds/Maltese, Bucks Point and Honiton-type laces and are designed to suit a range of abilities) are accompanied by working diagrams and instructions for making up the completed items. I have assumed that you are already conversant with the techniques involved in making the type of lace being worked; detailed instructions for the needlework techniques and stitches used can be found in my previous book, *Mounting and Using Lace*.

In most cases I have suggested alternative uses for both the prickings and the basic patterns. All the lace illustrated in this book was designed for its specific purpose, but you could use your favourite prickings (or design your own) for many of the items, which range from those involving very small amounts of lace through to more ambitious projects.

Before you start

Before starting on a piece of work, read through all the instructions so that you have an idea of what you are trying to achieve. Do not be put off a particular project because you do not make the type of lace indicated; in many cases, other suitable prickings could be substituted – for example, the collar illustrated in Fig. 77 could be made up in a much finer fabric and edged with a fine Bucks Point lace, or the jabot illustrated in Fig. 66 could be made with a fine Torchon edging.

The method for making up each item is included; full details of any methods and stitches mentioned but not described in detail may be found in *Mounting and Using Lace*. The thread used for each piece of lace is given only as a guide; you may prefer to use a different thread of a similar thickness. Make sure that it will wash successfully – to avoid disappointment, it is always worth making up a sample of the lace in your chosen thread and stitching it to a piece of the fabric. Wash this in the same way as you intend to wash the finished item, and check that you are happy with the result. Some threads will be much more successful than others.

I have assumed a working knowledge of each type of lace included, but a few notes on some of the techniques used are given below, and a working diagram is included for each pricking. On all these diagrams, one line represents a pair of threads unless otherwise stated. The diagrams also indicate the best position to start in order to obtain a neat join; this is not always the most obvious place (see Fig. 85). An arrow above a pinhole indicates that a pair or pairs should be hung on a temporary pin above that pinhole; the direction of the arrow shows the direction from which the threads enter the lace, and the number beside it indicates the number of pairs introduced at that pin. Where there is a number with no arrow close to a pinhole, that number of pairs are to be hung on that pin, which is *not* temporary. For example, refer to Fig. 35; begin the cloth stitch section by hanging five pairs of passives side by side on a temporary pin above, and one pair on each temporary pin on the left-hand side. One pair (to be used as weavers for this section) is hung directly on to the pin on the right-hand side of the trail. The footside edge is begun by hanging two pairs on a temporary pin directly above the first edge stitch to be worked, and one pair is hung on a temporary pin above and to the left. These three pairs then make the first edge stitch.

When working a closed border, such as for a handkerchief or traycloth, deciding where to begin and how to finish off neatly can worry many lacemakers. Before commencing work, decide where the neatest join can be made, and start the lace so that it may be joined in this position. The working diagrams for the prickings (except those in Figs 10, 12 and 14) indicate where to start in order to achieve this, and will repay careful study even if you do not intend to work the lace, as sometimes the best starting place is not obvious. Also bear in mind that not all patterns will enable an invisible join to be made, as in the prickings in Figs 9, 11 and 13.

Before starting to work a closed border, the following points are worth considering:

1) If possible, always start with the largest areas of cloth stitch or the largest areas surrounded by gimp threads, as the maximum number of threads can then be dealt with where they will not show.

2) In Beds/Maltese-type patterns, try to introduce pairs where they join into trails if possible. If they must be introduced at 'windmill', six- or eight-plait crossings, try to choose those where leaves rather than half-stitch plaits connect, so that the ends can be rolled behind the leaves.

3) Avoid starting in the centre of one side or right on a corner, as the join will be more conspicuous in these positions. On some patterns (particularly Bucks Point-type), however, the corner is the only place where the ground is completely cut by a gimp thread, and for this reason is the best place to start.

4) Avoid starting with large areas of ground or half-stitch where there is no gimp thread, because it is very difficult to make a join here which can be hidden. This makes it impossible to join some patterns invisibly; these are best used where the ends of the lace are not to be joined but can be hidden in a seam (for example, the lace on the cushion illustrated in Fig. 7).

5) When the ends of lace are to be hidden in a seam or binding, the starting position is unimportant and the ends can simply be finished by tying each pair in a reef knot and cutting off close to the knots.

When you are ready to join the lace, bear the following points in mind:

1) Pin the first part of the lace down firmly and accurately, pushing the pins right down into the pillow. Pin down *at least* one pattern repeat to avoid pulling the lace out of shape whilst taking the 'sewings'. Remember that it is better to pin back too much than too little; areas of half stitch and ground can easily pull out of

shape for quite a long way back. It is usually easier to do this in advance, covering the pinheads with either a cover cloth or a transparent piece of acetate to avoid snagging the working threads. If the lace is not pinned back until the last moment, it can be difficult to see the pinholes because of the working threads lying over them, although there are occasions when this is unavoidable – for example, see the bridal head-dress on page 67.

2) Make sure that any pairs which need to be twisted are twisted before taking the 'sewings'. Remove one pin at a time, take the 'sewing' and put back the pin *before* tying a reef knot. The 'sewings' may be made with either a fine hook or the eye of a needle (preferably bent and mounted in a handle) containing a short length of thread. In Honiton lace, 'sewings' are best taken with a needlepin, which can sometimes be used successfully for other fine laces. Whichever method is chosen, make sure that the tool used is fine enough to pass through the pinholes of the lace without stretching and distorting them. To avoid bulk, sew only one pair at a time.

3) It is usually necessary to lengthen each thread to make the 'sewings' possible. After tying, leave the thread on the bobbins for a little while; the weight will help to straighten the threads, which may then be cut off, leaving sufficient length to be threaded into a needle later. Gimp threads are neither sewn nor tied. When joining wide pieces or squares of lace (as in Fig. 84), it is often easier to 'sew' pairs in as they are finished with rather than waiting until all the lace has been completed. The threads can always be left to be tied later if you are concerned that you may need to undo your lace. The ends of thread are usually more easily dealt with after attaching the lace to the fabric, when those from the edge may be darned into the hem or stitching rather than into the lace.

4) Threads which have been joined into cloth stitch areas may be darned into the back of the cloth stitch, following the weave of the threads. On fine laces with a gimp, form the threads into one or more rolls which may be stitched to the back of the gimp. If possible, it is better to form several small rolls in different directions rather than one large one, so that the join will be less bulky. On Beds/Maltese-type patterns, the ends of the threads may be darned into the back of cloth-stitch trails or formed into small rolls which may be stitched to the back of leaves.

The following reminders on techniques may be useful when working these patterns.

1) a) **Hanging on pairs round a pin** (see Fig. 1a). It is essential to use this method when pairs are being introduced at windmill crossings and six- or eight-plait crossings, where each pair will be used as a single bobbin. It is also the best method when the two pairs will leave the pinhole in opposite directions, in order to be sure that the threads are connected.

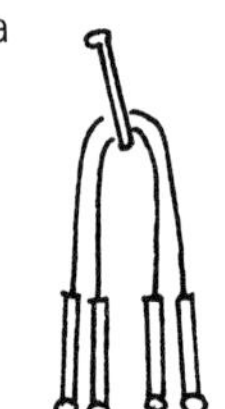

Fig. 1
a Hanging pairs round a pin

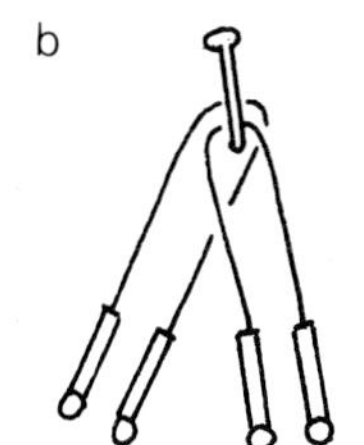

b Hanging pairs side by side

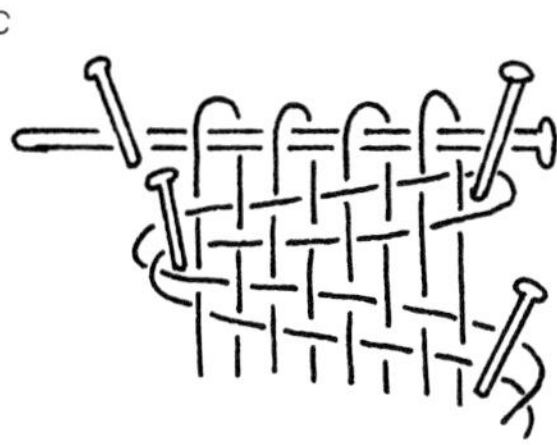

c Starting a trail or scallop

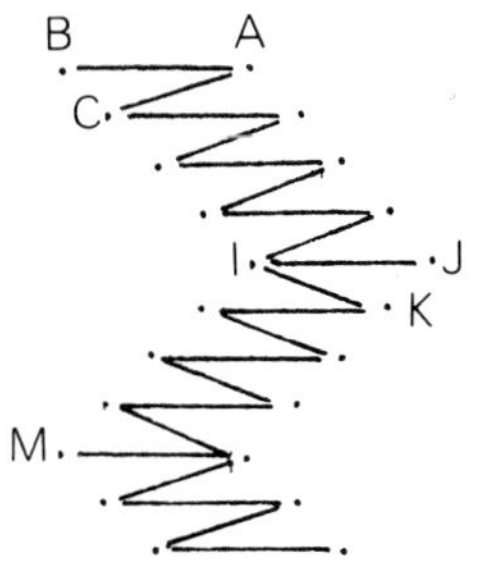

Fig. 2 Changing the weavers for a half-stitch trail, when the trail changes direction

b) **Hanging pairs on a pin side by side** (see Fig. 1b). Use this method when each pair must lie side by side in the lace, as when starting a trail or scallop.

c) **When starting a trail or scallop,** the passives are hung side by side on a temporary pin, and the first few rows worked. Instead of completely removing the temporary pin holding the starting passives, gently lift it from the pinhole, making sure that all the loops of thread are still held on it. Lay this pin across the pillow, supported at each end by the first pins used in working the trail, making sure that no threads are crossed and that they lie side by side as illustrated in Fig. 1c. Pull the passives down gently so that each loop of thread lies snugly round the laid pin. This method will provide a tiny loop for sewing out each pair of passives, making the joining of the lace much easier and also removing any danger of the weavers being pulled out of shape.

2) **When working half stitch trails in Torchon lace,** a more even result is obtained by changing the weavers for the trail each time it changes direction. The following method was used for all those samples including a half stitch trail which are illustrated.

Referring to Fig. 2, begin working the trail with the weavers on pin **A**. Work to pin **B**, which is then closed with a half stitch and the pairs left. Now pick up the last passive pair on the right-hand side of the trail (at **A**) and use these as new weavers to work to pin **C**. Using the same weaver, continue the trail to pin **J**, which is then closed with a half stitch.

When the next section of the trail is to be worked, pick up the last pair of passives on the left-hand side of the trail (at **I**) and use them as weavers to work towards pin **K**. Work the rest of the trail to pin **M**, where the pin is closed with a half stitch. For the next section of the trail, pick up the last pair of passives on the right-hand side as new weavers.

3) **Connecting plaits or leaves to footside or trails to leave immediately.** Referring to Fig. 3, bring the weavers through the passives and on through the two incoming pairs in cloth stitch. Set the pin *under* the weavers and *between* the two incoming pairs. Leave the weavers to go out for the next plait or leaf and use the two incoming pairs to close the pin with a cloth stitch. The pair nearest the trail now become the weavers.

Fig. 3 Connecting plaits or leaves to footside or trails to leave immediately:
a On the left
b On the right

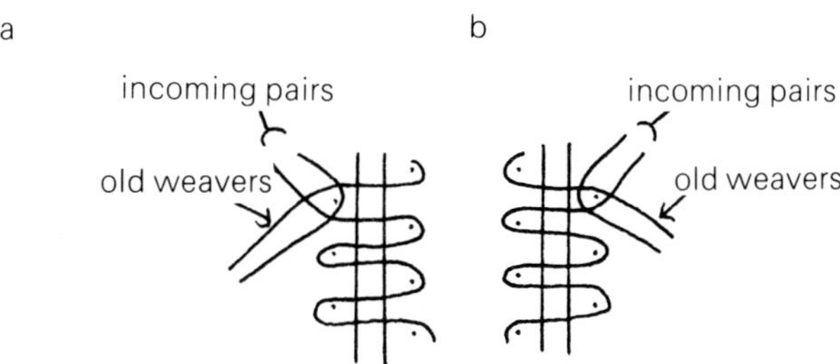

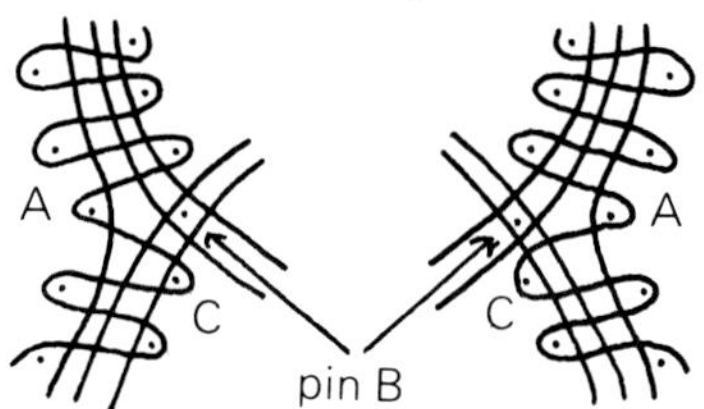

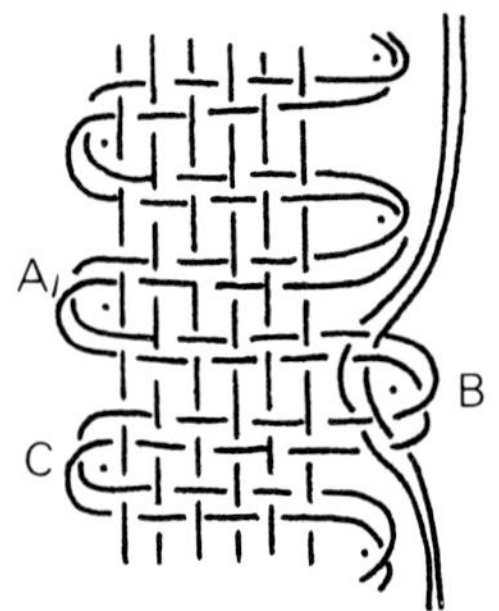

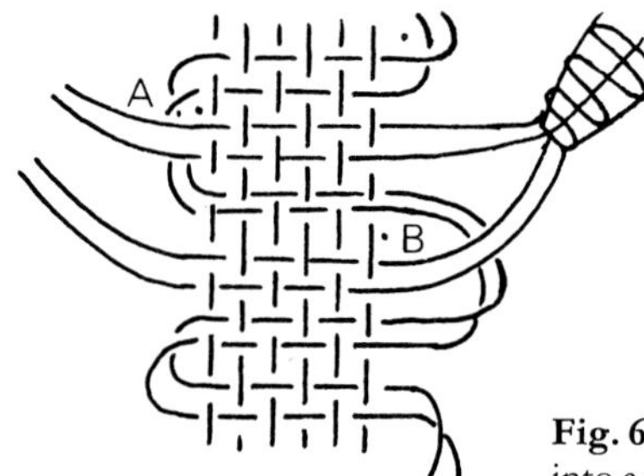

Fig. 4 Connecting plaits or leaves to a scallop to leave immediately:
a On the left
b On the right

Fig. 5 Introducing two new pairs at a pin

Fig. 6 Taking out two pairs into a trail

4) **Connecting plaits or leaves to a scallop to leave immediately**. Referring to Fig. 4a, work the scallop as far as **A** where the weavers are left hanging. Take the left-hand pair from the plait or leaf in cloth stitch through the two pairs of passives on the right-hand side of the scallop. Set pin **B** *under* the pair from the plait or leaf and *between* the two pairs of passives. Now pick up the right-hand pair from the plait or leaf and work it in cloth stitch through the same two pairs of passives. Return to the scallop weavers left at **A** and use them to work to pin **C**. The two pairs from the plait or leaf have now become scallop passives and the two scallop passive pairs will be left out to make the next plait or leaf. Note that the scallop weavers are *not* used to work pin **B**. This method forms a small hole, and the appearance of the lace is improved if a twisted vein is worked two pairs in from the right-hand side of the scallop. For a scallop on the right-hand side of the lace, follow the above instructions, reading 'right' for 'left' and vice-versa, and referring to Fig. 4b.

5) **Introducing two new pairs at a pin**. Referring to Fig. 5, work the trail as usual to pin **A** and then lay two pairs of bobbins across the pillow from front to back on the opposite side of the trail. Work from **A** through the trail passives and on in cloth stitch through the two bobbins at the front of the pillow. Set pin **B** under the weavers and work back to pin **C** through the same pairs, then continue the trail as before. The two new threads lying at the back of the pillow can now be brought forward to where they are required.

6) **Taking out two pairs into a trail**. This method allows the original passives to be retained, making an even trail. Referring to Fig. 6, work the trail to pin **A** where the weavers are left; take the left-hand pair from the plait or leaf through the trail passives as if they were weavers and lay them to the back of the pillow to be tied and cut off later. Bring the trail weavers at pin **A** through the passives, set pin **B** under them and leave them. Now bring the second pair from the plait or leaf over the weavers without making a stitch, and then work them through the trail passives, finally laying them to the back to be tied and cut off later. Now resume working the trail with its original weavers.

Alternative uses are suggested for most of the prickings given. When they are to be lengthened, make copies by either photocopying or pricking through several layers of paper, and then join them carefully and accurately. When planning lace to fit a particular size (e.g. for the neckline of the blouse illustrated in Fig. 102) it is often useful to prepare a pricking and then make several rubbings of it, which can be glued together to enable the exact number of pattern repeats to be calculated.

Some of the suggestions involve changing the scale of the lace; in this case remember to change the weight of thread to suit. If a suitable machine is available, photocopying is the easiest method for changing the scale of a pattern, but remember that photocopiers can cause distortion and that, when enlarging, they will also enlarge the spots and any slight errors. Greater accuracy will be achieved by working the design out on a suitably-sized grid, but this is far more time-consuming.

Striped cushion

This is a combination of lace and simple drawn-thread work, which would be ideal for a first attempt at drawn-thread work. The finished size is approximately 41 cm (16 inches) square, but this could easily be altered. The original was worked in blue with a navy-blue lining.

The cushion is illustrated in Fig. 7, and a detail of the lace is shown in Fig. 8.

Fig. 7 Striped cushion

Fig. 8 Detail of cushion shown in Fig. 7

Materials Brilliante d'Alsace No. 30 – 26 pairs of bobbins for the pricking in Fig. 9, 18 pairs for the pricking in Fig. 11 and 14 pairs for the pricking in Fig. 13

DMC Perle No. 8 two single gimp bobbins for each pricking. In the sample illustrated, this was a slightly deeper colour thread

Evenweave linen (to match the lace) with 29 threads to the inch – 44 cm (17¼ inches) by 39 cm (15½ inches); evenweave cotton with 27 threads to the inch would be equally suitable

Cotton fabric 44 cm (17¼ inches) square to line the front of the cushion

Fabric suitable for back of the cushion and to cover piping cord – 44 cm (17¼ inches) by 84 cm (33 inches); I used a matching shade of Needlecord, but the same evenweave fabric could be used

Piping cord – 180 cm (two yards). This should be washed before use to shrink it

A zip, if required, to close the back

Tapestry needle No. 24

The lace The ends of each strip of lace will later be enclosed in a seam, so they can be started where convenient and finished by tying each pair in a reef knot. The prickings and working diagrams are given in Figs 9 to 14.

Remember to change the weavers in the half stitch trails to keep them even (see note 2 on page 11). Hold the gimp in place on the inner corners of the trails (indicated * on Figs 10 and 14) by passing it through the weavers, then twist the weavers once and pass the gimp back through them. Continue in the usual way. You will require one length of lace made on the pricking in Fig. 9, and two each made on the prickings in Figs 11 and 13, all about 44 cm (17¼ inches) long.

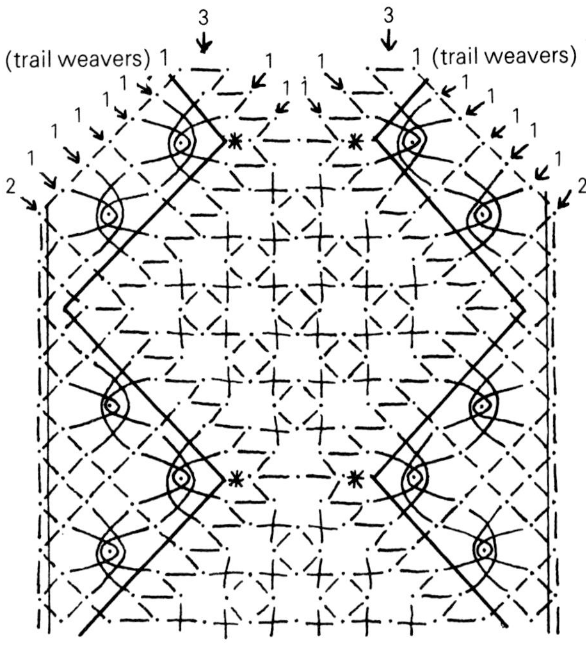

Fig. 9 Pricking for cushion shown in Fig. 7

Fig. 10 Working diagram for pricking in Fig. 9. Introduce two single gimps where shown

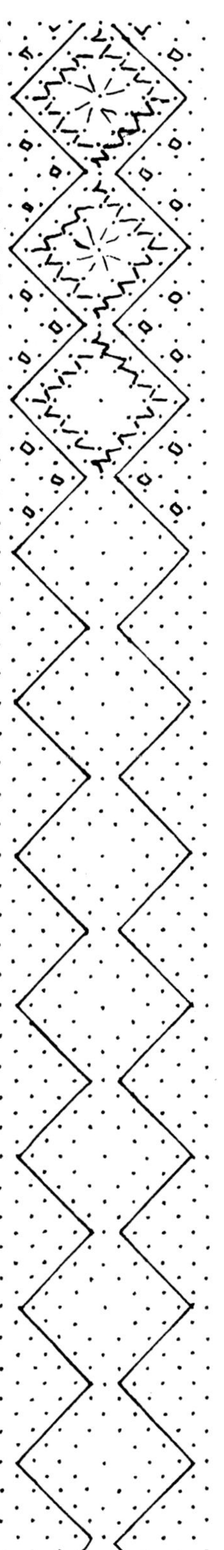

Fig. 11 Pricking for cushion
illustrated in Figs 7 and 8

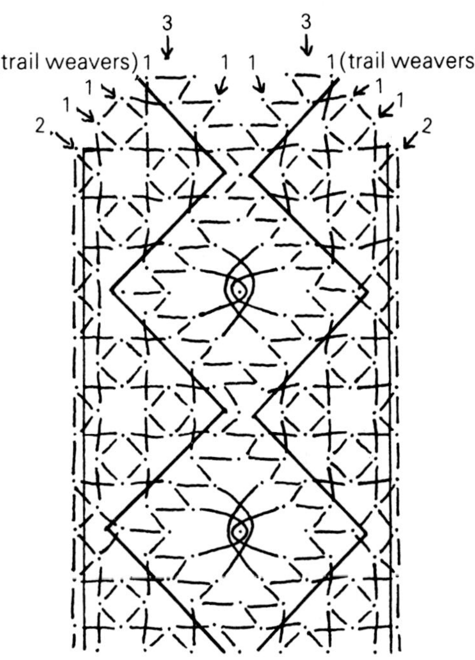

Fig. 12 Working diagram for
pricking in Fig. 11. Introduce
two single gimps where
shown

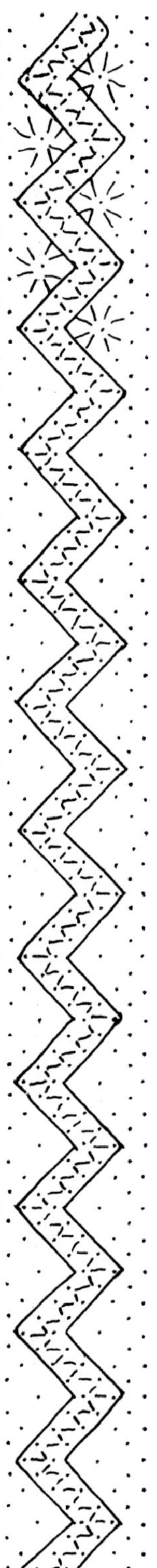

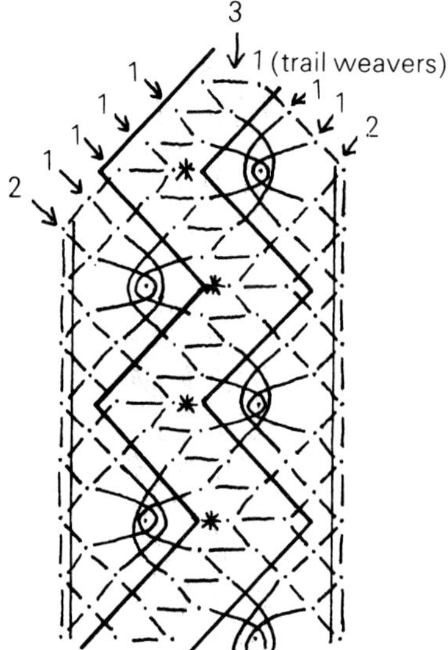

Fig. 14 Working diagram for
pricking in Fig. 13. Introduce
two single gimps where
shown

a Withdraw threads as shown

b Make double fold hems on long sides

a

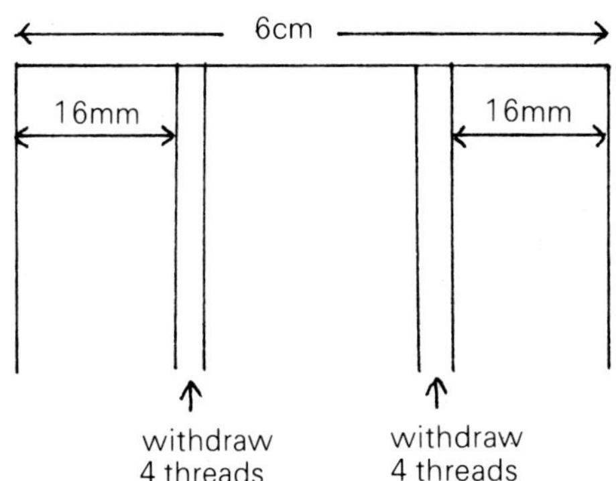

b

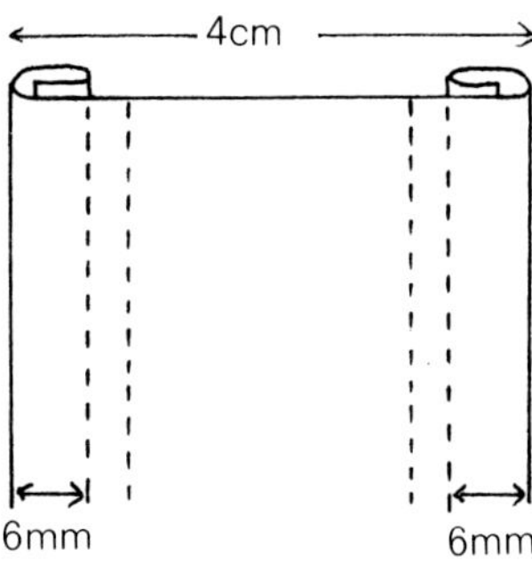

Drawn-thread work Cut four strips of fabric 44 cm (17¼ inches) by 6 cm (2⅜ inches). Withdraw four threads as shown in Fig. 15a and prepare 6 mm (¼ inch) deep double-fold hems along both long edges of each strip, finished width 4 cm (1½ inches). Stitch the hems into place using zig-zag or ladder hem-stitch and bunching the threads in groups of four. Then cut two strips 44 cm (17¼ inches) by 7.5 cm (3 inches) and make a hem along one long edge of each strip in the same way. These two strips are for the outer sides of the cushion, and their unhemmed edges will be incorporated in the side seams.

Making up Referring to Fig. 7, flat overcast the lace into place on the hemmed edges of the fabric. Now place the lace and linen on to the lining and tack together around the edges. If required, the back may be fastened with a zip, which should be inserted before making up. Finally, make up the cushion using the piping cord.

Alternatives Because of the half-stitch trails, lace worked on these prickings is not easy to join neatly and is therefore not very adaptable. However, the prickings in Figs 9 and 11 could be adapted for use as bookmarks if you started and finished with a diamond shape; they could also be used on a blouse where the ends can be incorporated into a seam.

Suitable alternative prickings into which embroidery ribbon can be threaded (see the bookmark on page 46) could also be used. If slightly wider bands of ladder hem stitch are worked on the fabric, these can be threaded with the same ribbon.

Place setting

The lace was made in ecru to match the serviette (finished size 30 cm [12 inches] square) and mounted on dusky pink fabric. The placemat measures 39 cm ($15\frac{1}{4}$ inches) by 29 cm ($11\frac{1}{2}$ inches).

The complete place setting is illustrated in Fig. 16 and a detail of the lace in Fig. 17.

Fig. 16 Place setting

Fig. 17 Detail of lace shown in Fig. 16

Materials Tanne cotton No. 30 – 21 pairs of bobbins for the small motif and 28 pairs for the large motif

Cotton fabric 52 cm (20½ inches) by 34 cm (13½ inches) for the place-mat and serviette ring

Lining fabric 16 cm (6¼ inches) square for the serviette ring

Cotton fabric 34 cm (13½ inches) square for the serviette

Small piece of iron-on interfacing

One press-stud

The large motif To work the motif, refer to Figs 18 and 19 and notes 1(a) on page 10, 1(b), 1(c) and 3 on page 11, notes 4 and 5 on page 12 and note 6 on page 13. Take out two pairs at each pin marked with an **X** in Fig. 19. To complete the motif, the pairs from the scallop and trail may be darned into the cloth stitch, and the remaining pairs form small rolls up the back of adjacent leaves.

Fig. 18 Pricking for lace shown in Fig. 16

Fig. 19 Working diagram for pricking in Fig. 18

The small motif　The small motif is made in the same way (and on the same pricking) as the large motif, but omitting the outer scalloped edge and also the leaves between the scallops and trail. The outer edge of this motif is then worked with a footside edge stitch. The ends of thread may be left to be darned through to the back of the fabric.

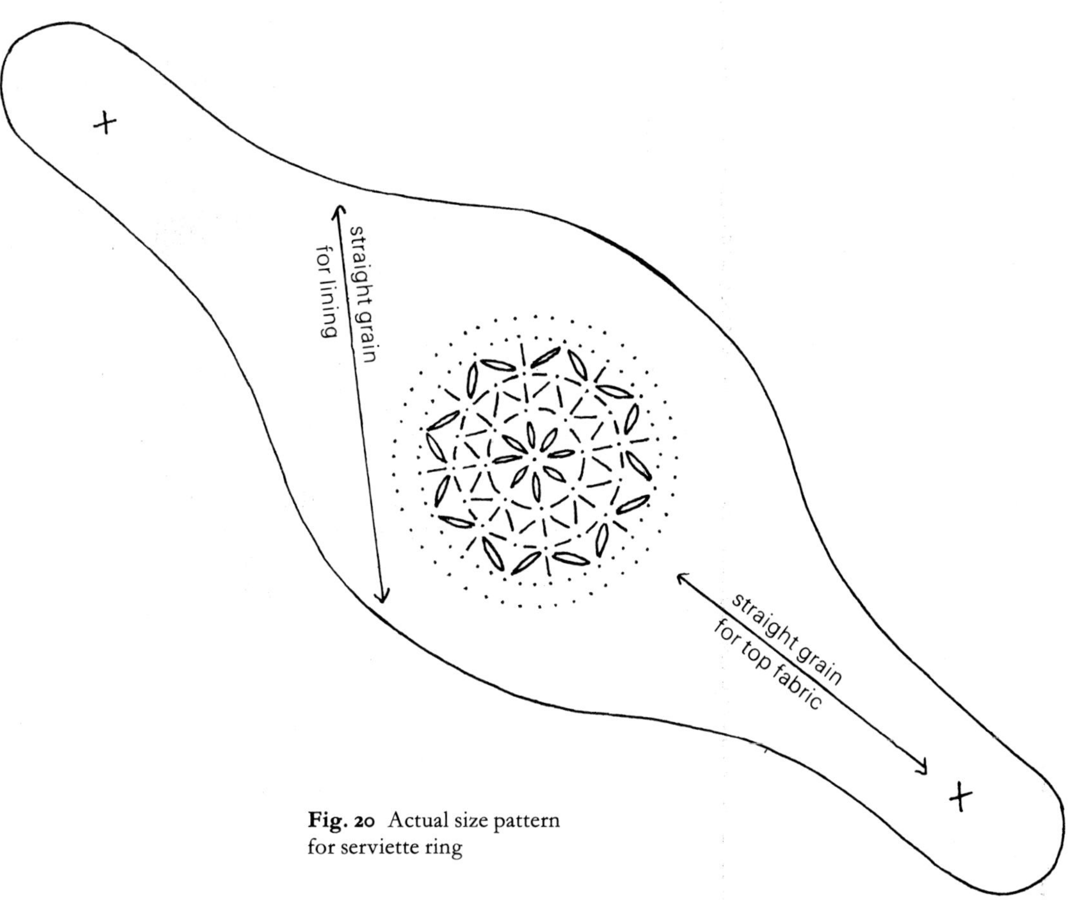

Fig. 20 Actual size pattern for serviette ring

Making up the serviette	This is simply finished with a drawn-thread hem, remembering to mitre the corners. One corner could be trimmed with the smaller motif, made in the same colour as the place-mat.
Making up the place-mat	Because the weave of the cotton fabric used was close, the hem was pin-stitched in place, withdrawing one fabric thread as a guide to keep the stitching true to the grain. Remember to mitre the corners. Finish off all the threads of the lace before stitching the motif into place in the corner, about 1 cm ($\frac{3}{8}$ inch) from the hem. On the original it was stitched invisibly into place, but pin stitch could also have been used, following the outline of the motif.
Making up the serviette ring	Cut two shapes from iron-on interfacing using the pattern given in Fig. 20. Iron one shape on to the wrong side of the fabric, checking that the grain runs down the shape as shown (the grain line and position of the motif can be drawn lightly on to the interfacing before ironing, to ensure accurate placing). Make sure that there is at

least 6 mm ($\frac{1}{4}$ inch) excess fabric all round the shape. Invisibly stitch the motif into place, making sure it is central, and darn all the thread ends through to the back of the fabric. Now iron on the second piece of interfacing, trapping all the ends and making sure it is in exactly the same place as the first (if this is still not stiff enough, a third layer can be ironed on).

Now trim the excess fabric away, leaving about 6 mm ($\frac{1}{4}$ inch) all round. Clip the allowance at intervals all round and fold to the wrong side, over the interfacing, keeping the fabric flat. Tack into place and then press.

The lining is prepared by cutting the given shape from thin card and then trimming off 1.5 mm ($\frac{1}{16}$ inch) all the way round. Cut (on the bias, from either the same or a different fabric) and tack the lining to the card in the same way as the front was tacked to the interfacing. Press to set the folded edge, remove the tacking and carefully remove the card without disturbing the creased edge. Place the lining into position on the serviette ring and slip-stitch the two together. Remove the tacking threads and fasten with a press-stud in the position marked by a cross on the pattern.

Alternatives

1) Different motifs (especially Honiton) could be used to make a set of serviette rings.
2) The larger motif will fit into a 75-mm (3-inch) trinket box or frame, but would look more delicate if worked in Tanne No. 50. In this case you would need to increase the number of pairs in the trail.
3) The smaller motif could also be inserted or applied to a handkerchief – it is illustrated inserted into a handkerchief on page 44 of *Mounting and Using Lace*.
4) Several motifs could be placed round the front edges of a waistcoat or jacket, the edges of which could be scalloped to match.

Traycloth with pulled-thread work

Fig. 21 Traycloth with
pulled-thread work

Pulled-thread work lends itself well to being combined with Torchon lace. The pattern effects are gained by pulling stitches tightly to open up holes in the evenweave fabric, not by withdrawing threads from the fabric. Many variations are possible; for example, the satin-stitch blocks can be worked in various directions and different tensions to give a variety of effects. These fillings can be worked into a variety of shapes, not necessarily geometric; for example, in a Beds/Maltese-type pattern with a heart-shape in the design, these shapes could be echoed on the fabric.

The original traycloth, which was worked on a cream-coloured fabric, is approximately 56 cm (22 inches) by 44 cm ($17\frac{1}{4}$ inches) including the lace. It is illustrated in Fig. 21, and a detail of the lace and embroidery is shown in Fig. 22.

Materials Campbells Linen No. 60 (or equivalent, e.g. Tanne No. 12) – 30 pairs of bobbins
Evenweave cotton fabric (27 threads to the inch) 48 cm (19 inches) by 36 cm ($14\frac{1}{4}$ inches)
Perle No. 12 and Brilliante d'Alsace No. 30 to match fabric
Tapestry needle No. 24

The lace Referring to Figs 23 and 24, start at the top of the cloth stitch diamond. The pattern includes rose ground, snowflake filling, spiders and a twisted Torchon fan (twist weavers twice and passives

Fig. 22 Detail of traycloth shown in Fig. 21

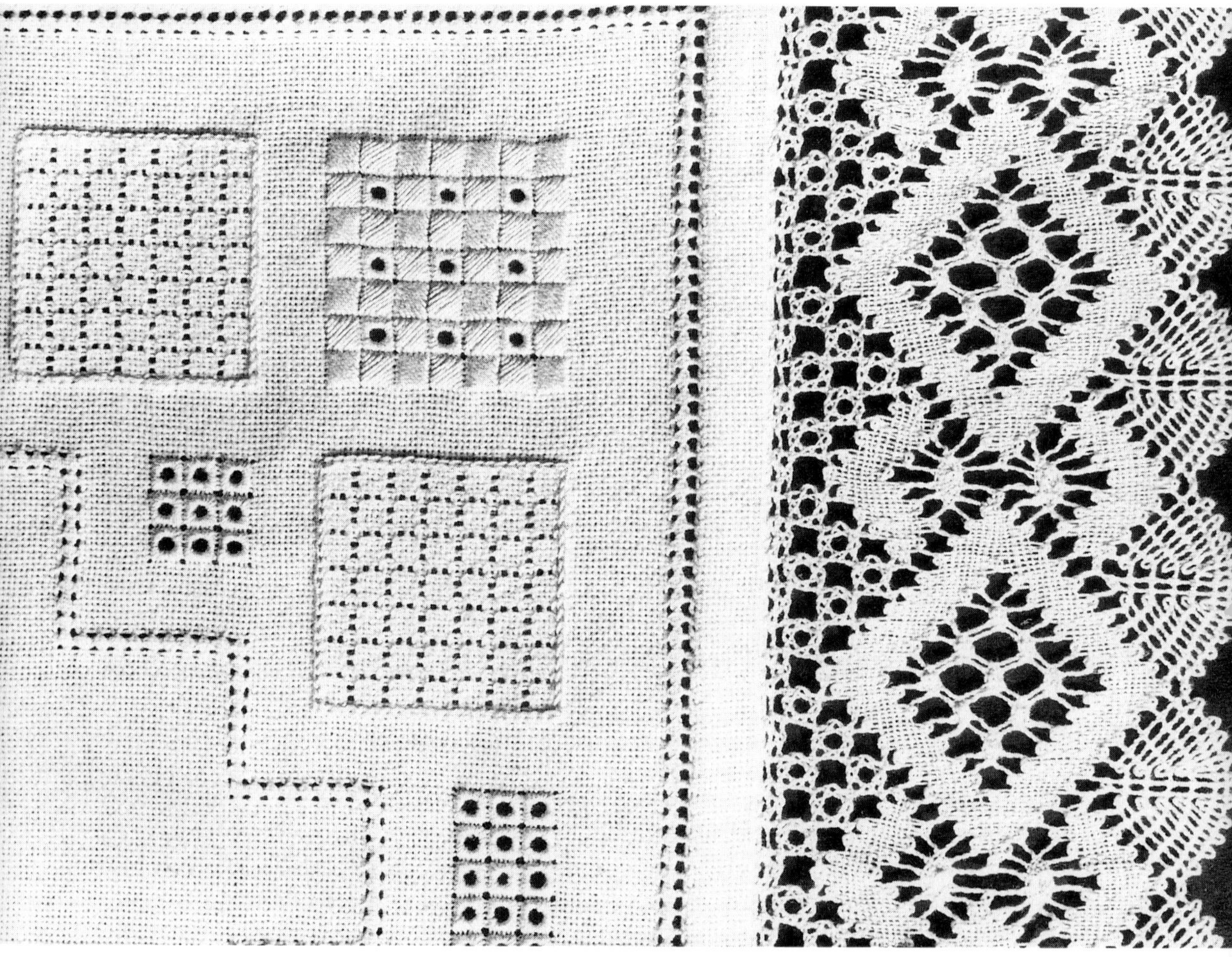

26

once). To finish neatly, most threads are darned into the cloth stitch. Two pairs will need to be overcast to the back of the fan and the edge pairs may be darned into the hem. The two pairs from the rose ground should be darned into the ground as neatly as possible to carry them across to the footside where they can be darned away into the hem.

The embroidery   This should be worked after making the lace. Place the lace on the fabric following the straight grain exactly and tack just inside the footside edge to mark its position (and therefore the finished size of the fabric). Also tack lines to mark the centre of the fabric in both directions.

Referring to Fig. 25a, mark the positions for the embroidery by tacking in the squares (count under and over three threads for each stitch to make this easier). The exact length of each side can be altered to suit the size of the lace as indicated in Fig. 25a. Tack in the position of all the embroidery before starting it, as the embroidery stitches will mark the fabric and make it difficult to move an area of embroidery at a later stage if required.

The embroidery is best worked in a frame – it is easier to count the threads and maintain the tension. Start by making the eyelets in the smaller squares using Perle No. 12 and a tight tension to make the central hole. Each eyelet is worked over six threads (see Figs 22 and 26a).

The large corner squares are also worked in Perle No. 12. Referring to Figs 22 and 26b, firstly work satin-stitch blocks (in alternate directions) over six threads. The tension should be such that the thread lies smoothly without pulling holes in the fabric. Then work the eyelets in exactly the same way as for the smaller squares.

The remaining large squares are worked in ringed back stitch using Brilliante d'Alsace No. 30 – each stitch is made over two threads of fabric, pulling it tight as shown in Fig. 26c, d and e. Avoid joining in a new thread other than at the beginning or end of a row. Then neaten the outline of these squares by working a row of chain stitch (normal tension) in Perle No. 12.

The complete design is outlined in four-sided stitch, each stitch being made over three threads of the fabric (see Fig. 25a).

When the embroidery has been worked, check the position of the finished edge of the fabric and adjust the depth of hem if necessary, because the embroidery will tend to 'shrink' the material; I found it necessary when making the original to move the finished edge out by four threads all round at this stage. When the hem position has been finalised, withdraw one thread all round immediately next to the row of four-sided stitch and mitre the corners; make a simple drawn-thread hem, bunching the threads in groups of three. Finally, attach the lace and darn in the ends.

Fig. 23 Pricking for lace
illustrated in Figs 21 and 22

Fig. 24 Working diagram for pricking in Fig. 23

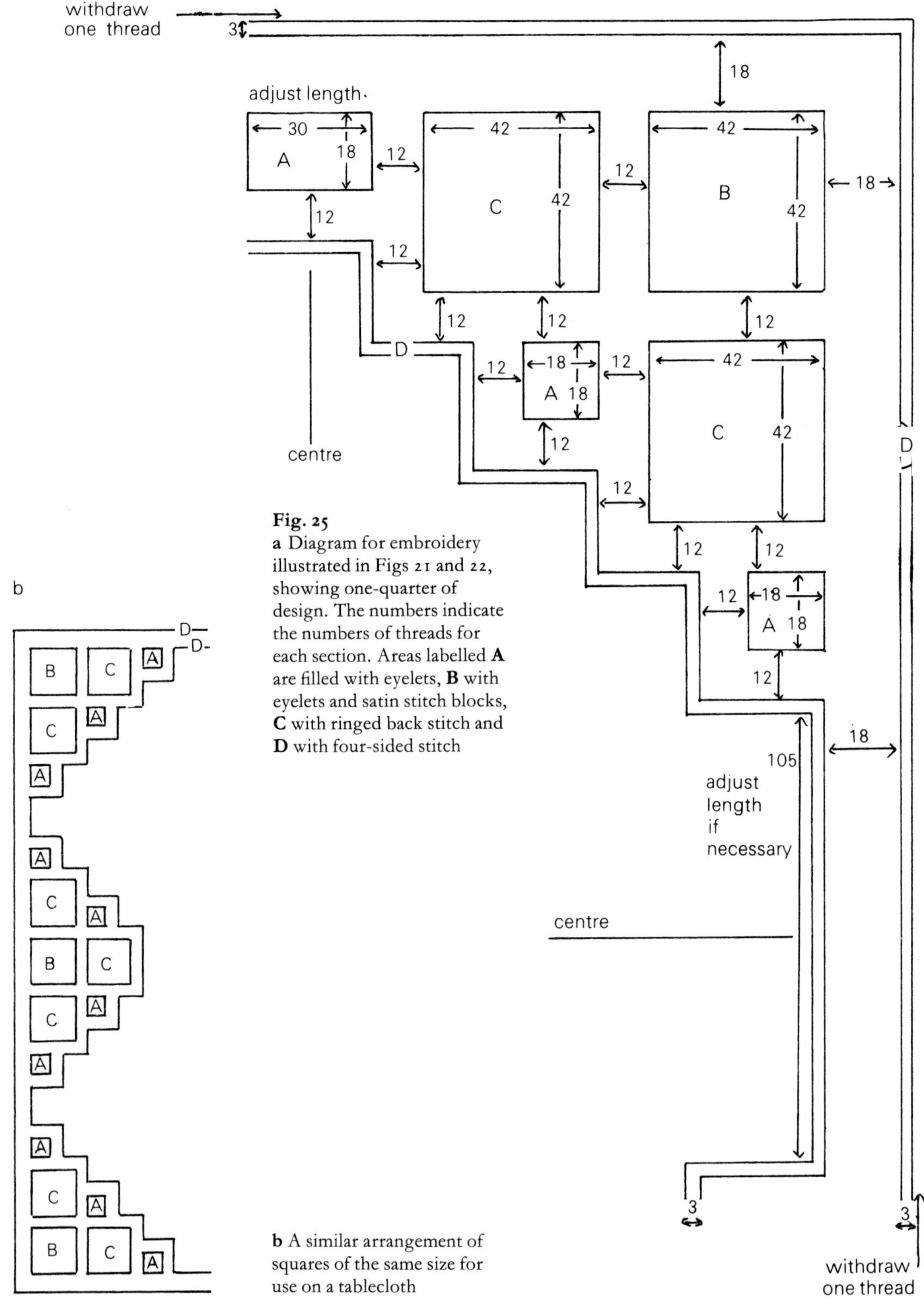

Fig. 25
a Diagram for embroidery illustrated in Figs 21 and 22, showing one-quarter of design. The numbers indicate the numbers of threads for each section. Areas labelled **A** are filled with eyelets, **B** with eyelets and satin stitch blocks, **C** with ringed back stitch and **D** with four-sided stitch

b A similar arrangement of squares of the same size for use on a tablecloth

Fig. 26 Stitches used for the embroidery illustrated in Fig. 22:

a

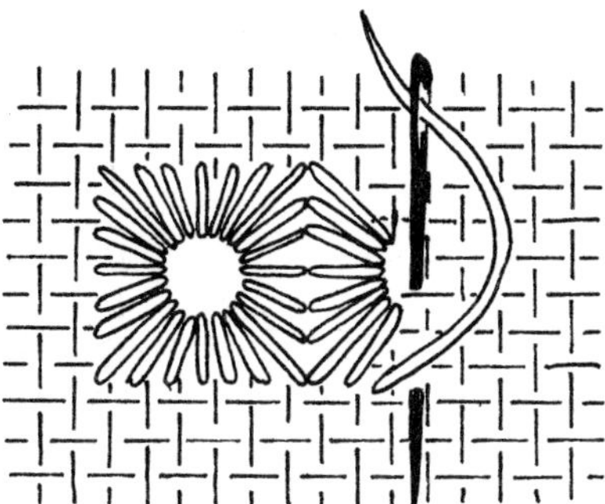

a Eyelets

b

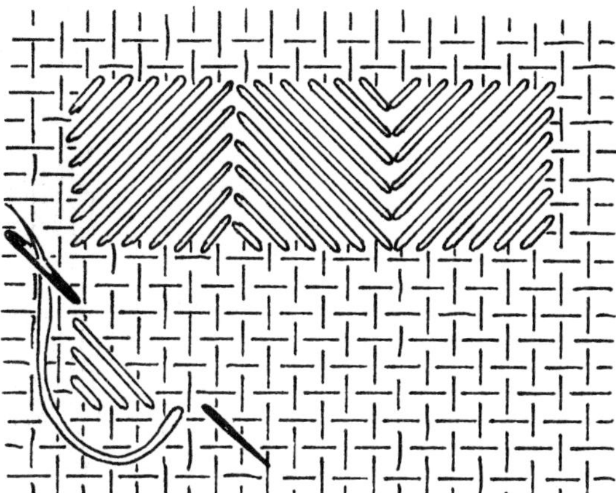

b Blocks of satin stitch

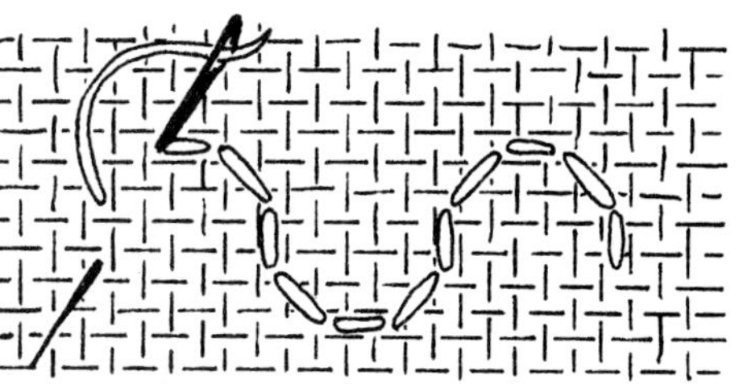

c First row of ringed back stitch

d

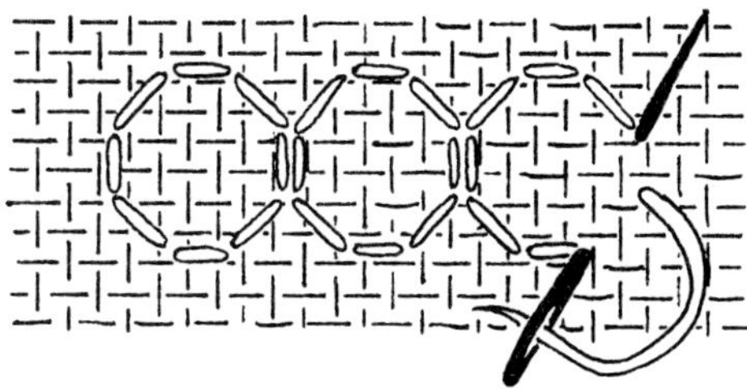

d Second row of ringed back stitch. Note that the vertical stitches are in the same spaces as the vertical stitches of the first row

e

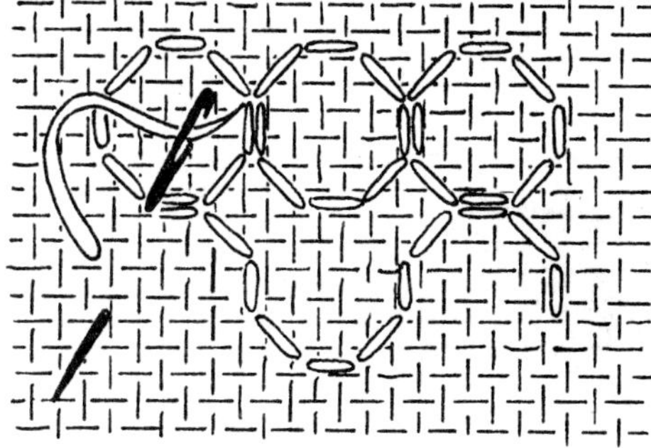

e Third row of ringed back stitch. Note that the upper horizontal stitches are in the same spaces as the lower horizontal stitches of the second row

Alternatives This embroidery design would also be suitable for use on a tablecloth (see Fig. 25b). The design size will vary if the fabric has a different number of threads to the inch.

On a finer grid, this edging would be most attractive on a handkerchief. The one illustrated on page 90 of *Mounting and Using Lace* was pricked diagonally on a 1/10-inch grid and worked in Bouc Linen No. 120.

Mat with counted-thread embroidery

Fig. 27 Mat with counted-thread embroidery

Fig. 28 Detail of mat shown in Fig. 27

This mat combines simple counted-thread embroidery with Torchon lace, which incorporates divided cloth stitch trails, snowflake filling (small spiders with no ground between), rose ground and a twisted Torchon fan. The original lace was worked in a pale green, with a darker green used for the fan weaver and the embroidery.

Its finished size is about 43 cm (17 inches) square. It is illustrated in Fig. 27, a detail of the lace and embroidery is shown in Fig. 28.

<table>
<tr><td>Materials</td><td>Tanne No. 30 – 37 pairs to match the fabric plus one pair (the fan weavers) in a deeper shade
Fine Aida (Hardanger) fabric with 18 blocks to the inch, 33 cm (13 inches) square
Stranded embroidery cotton to match fan weaver (two skeins)
Tapestry needle No. 24</td></tr>
<tr><td>The lace</td><td>If a fan weaver needs replacing when working with a different colour from the rest of the lace, it is necessary to work with a double thread on this bobbin for a short while. This is contrary to the usual rule, but successful because the number of twists on the thread will hold it securely and show only as a slight thickening.
　　Referring to Figs 29 and 30, begin by hanging pairs as indicated. The working is straightforward except for two pins at the centre of the snowflake filling. For each of these pins, only three pairs are available instead of the usual four. The single pair crosses through the other two in cloth stitch; put up a pin under it and then cross it</td></tr>
</table>

Fig. 29 Pricking for lace illustrated in Figs 27 and 28

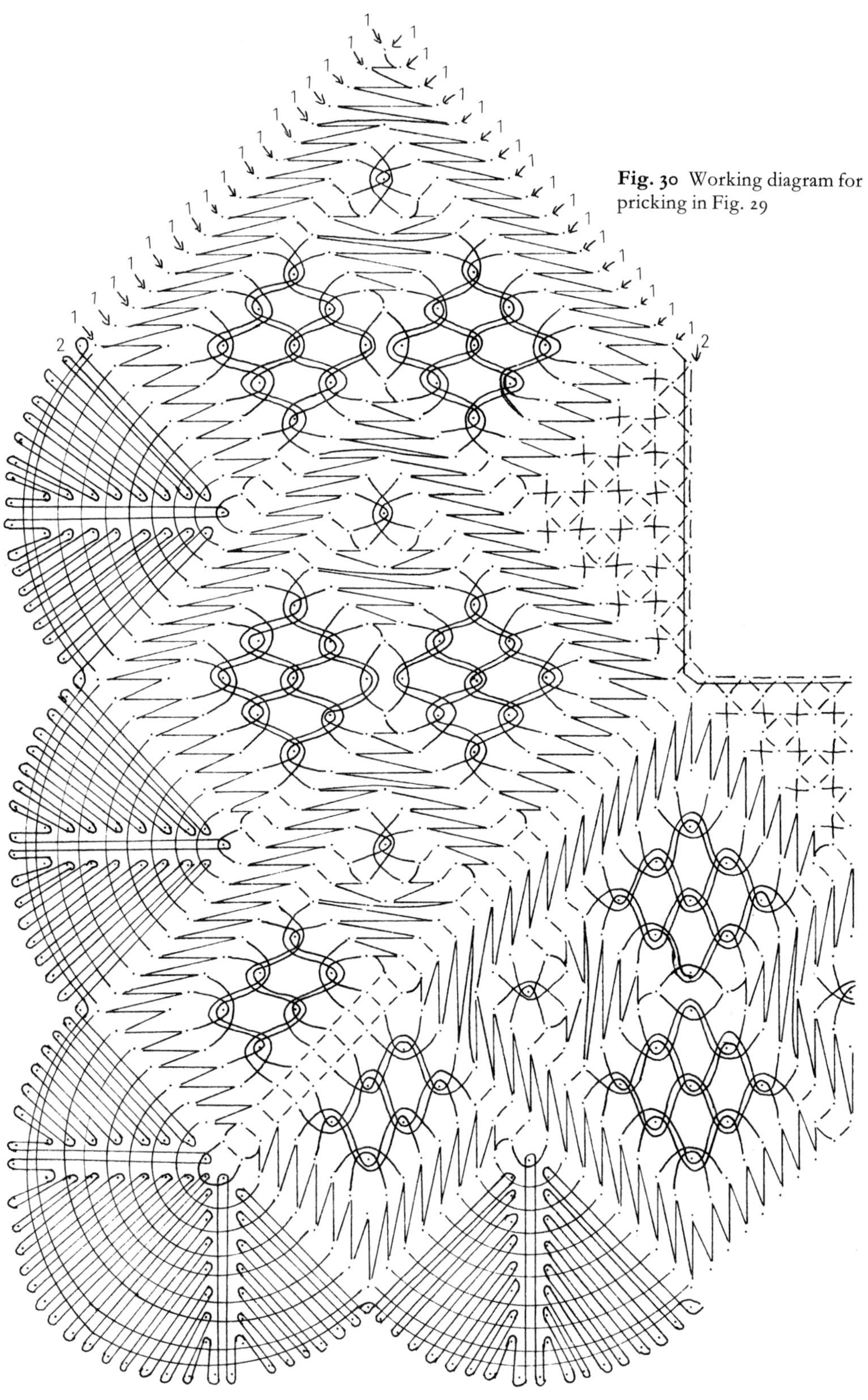

Fig. 30 Working diagram for pricking in Fig. 29

back to its original position (see Fig. 30).

To finish off neatly, all but four pairs may be darned away into the cloth stitch. Of these remaining pairs, two will be at the footside edge and may be darned into the hem; the others must be overcast to the back of the fan.

The embroidery

By tacking, mark the position of the finished hem to fit the lace and ensure that there is a multiple of four blocks plus two extra on each side (on the original $(51 \times 4) + 2 = 206$). Mark the centre lines by tacking and then work the embroidery starting from the centre line as shown on the chart in Fig. 31, noting that the diamonds should overlap in the same direction as those in the lace. The design is worked in back stitch using two strands of the cotton, each stitch being worked over one block of the fabric. One square on the chart represents one block of fabric. The crosses are worked last, over two blocks – make sure they all cross in the same direction. Do *not* work the triangular areas of four-sided stitch at this stage.

Making up

As the fabric is fairly stiff, a single-fold hem has been chosen to avoid bulk. Prepare the hem, mitring the corners. Leave one block of the fabric unworked all round the outer edge and then work three rows of four-sided stitch through both layers of the fabric. Work with Tanne No. 30 to match the fabric, making each stitch over two blocks. Cut away excess fabric at the back as close to the stitching as possible. Now work one more row of four-sided stitch all round (the number of rows may be adjusted if necessary). To complete the design, work the triangular shapes shown on the chart (Fig. 31) in four-sided stitch, continuing to space them evenly along each edge as far into the corners as possible. Finish the corners with a triangle as shown in Fig. 27, adjusting its size to fit the available space. Finally, overcast the lace into place and darn in the ends.

Alternatives

1) Finish with a simple double-fold hem.
2) Finish the hem as described under *Making up*, but omit the triangles.
3) This design could be used for place-mats, but to avoid fussiness work a band of embroidery along only one or both of the short sides, depending on the size of the finished mat.
4) A handsome tablecloth edging could be made by enlarging the pricking onto a 1/10-inch grid. This could be worked in either Tanne No. 12 or Campbells linen No. 60. This embroidery design could be adapted so that the diamond shapes are the same size as those in the lace; alternatively, the design could be interpreted for use on evenweave fabric in either counted-thread work or pulled-thread work. A different filling could be worked in each space and outlined with chain stitch – the design could also be extended by adding extra overlapping diamonds.
5) For a handkerchief edging, reduce the pricking to a 1/20-inch grid and work in Tanne No. 50 or Brilliante d'Alsace 50.

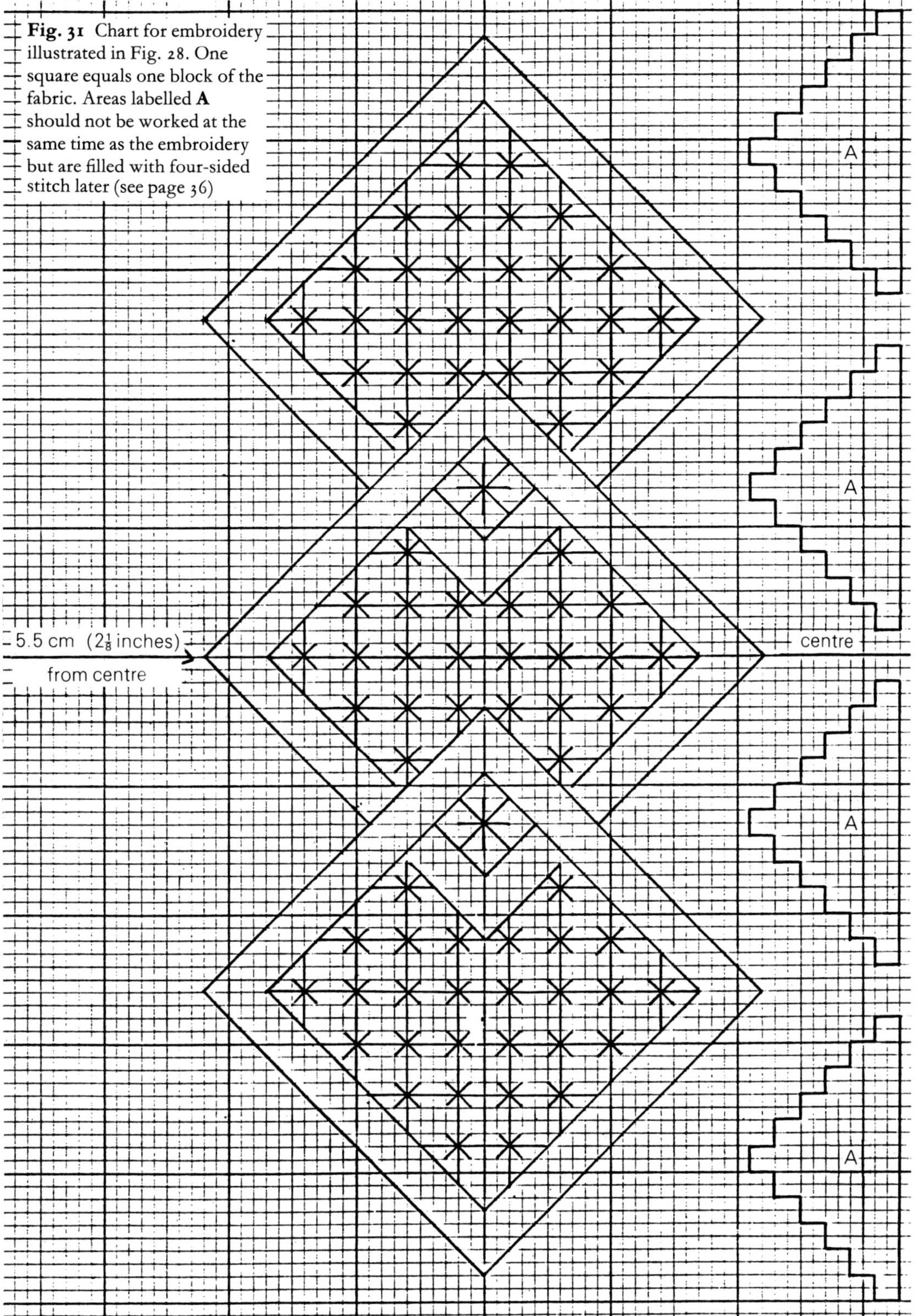

Fig. 31 Chart for embroidery illustrated in Fig. 28. One square equals one block of the fabric. Areas labelled **A** should not be worked at the same time as the embroidery but are filled with four-sided stitch later (see page 36)

Oval mat with shadow appliqué

Shadow appliqué gives a delicate appearance; the underlying fabric can be either white or coloured, and should not fray easily. It is also important that both fabrics should launder in the same way; I suggest that you wash them beforehand to check. For the original, white organdie and an old-rose coloured cotton fabric were chosen, and the lace was made in a colour to match the shadow. This technique would combine well with shadow-work embroidery.

The finished size is 42 cm (16½ inches) by 32.5 cm (12¾ inches), including lace. It is illustrated in Fig. 32, and a detail of the lace and embroidery is shown in Fig. 33.

Fig. 32 Oval mat with shadow appliqué

Fig. 33 Detail of mat shown in Fig. 32

Materials   Tanne No. 30, 19 pairs
Tanne No. 50 in same colour for the shadow appliqué
Piece of cotton organdie, 38 cm (15 inches) by 29 cm (11½ inches)
Piece of lightweight cotton fabric, 65 cm (25½ inches) by 29 cm (11½ inches)
Tapestry needle No. 24

The lace   Referring to Figs 34 and 35, begin by hanging pairs on temporary pins and work the cloth stitch trail, remembering to lay the temporary pin holding the five pairs of passives across the top of the trail after working a few rows (see note 1c on page 11). The working is fairly straightforward, but take particular care to note which areas are in cloth stitch and which in half stitch (see Fig. 32). On the half stitch shapes, remember to change the weavers (see note 2 on page 11) each time the trail changes direction. Work the scallop, twisting

as indicated in Fig. 35b where each dash indicates one twist. To
finish off, the three edge pairs may be darned into the hem of the mat,
and the remaining pairs are all darned into the cloth stitch trail.

For the oval mat illustrated, combine the prickings as shown in
Fig. 36a. For a longer runner, add repeats of Fig. 34b as many times
as required, noting that this pricking is one complete pattern repeat.

Fig. 34 Prickings for lace
illustrated in Figs 32 and 33:

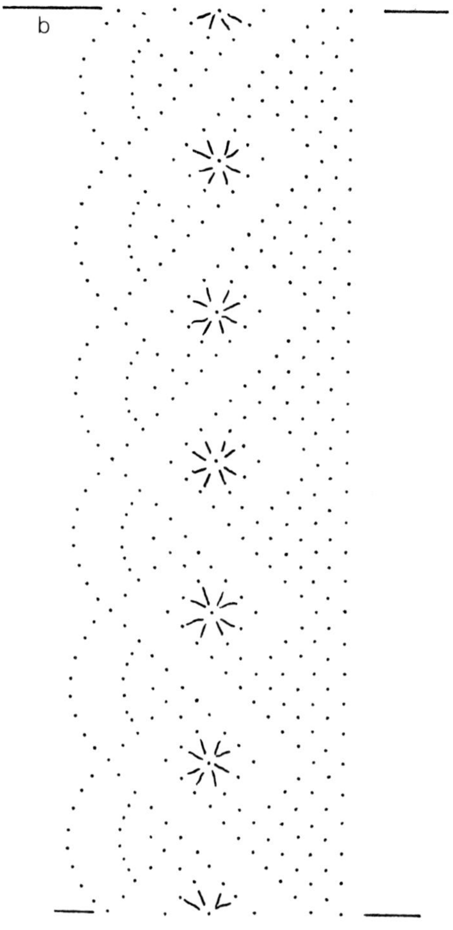

b One complete pattern
repeat

a 1/6 of a circle and one
complete pattern repeat

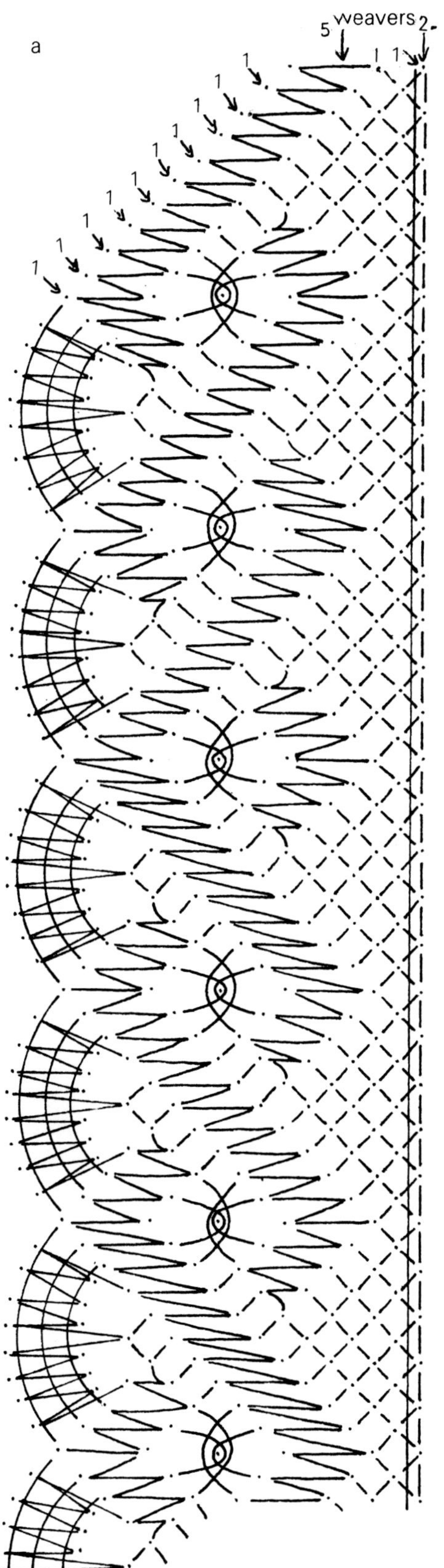

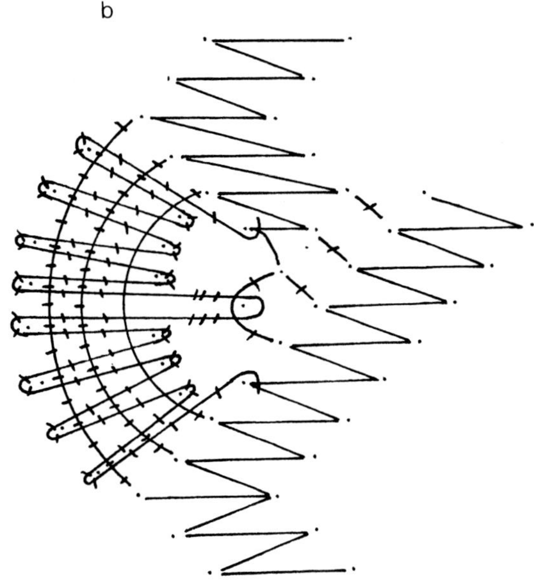

Fig. 35 Working diagram for prickings in Fig. 34. In **b**, each dash indicates that the pair is twisted

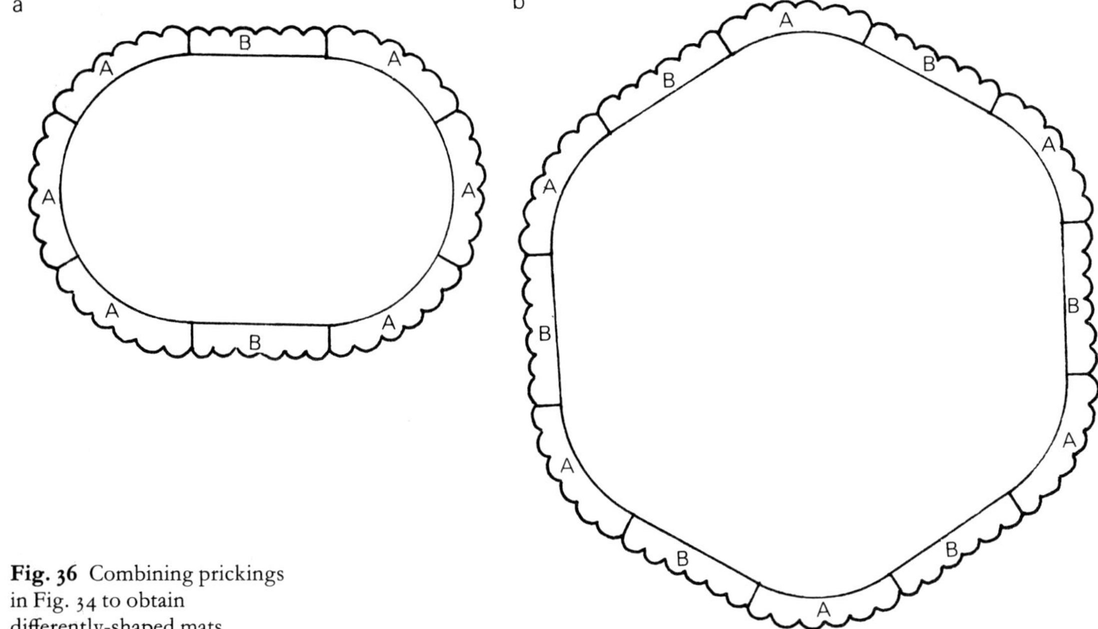

Fig. 36 Combining prickings
in Fig. 34 to obtain
differently-shaped mats

Shadow appliqué   By tacking, mark the centre of the organdie. Transfer the design given in Fig. 37 on to the organdie by tacking, with a water-erasable pen or with watercolour paint. Tack both layers together as shown in Fig. 38, making sure the grain of both fabrics is exactly in line and working all stitching from the centre outwards. Frame the fabric at this stage if preferred.

The design lines may be worked in pin stitch, three-sided stitch or four-sided stitch. However, pin stitch is likely to allow the fabric to pull away and three-sided stitch can appear rather heavy. For these reasons, four-sided stitch was chosen.

It was worked in a fine thread (Tanne No. 50) to match the colour of the lace, because, while the stitching should be inconspicuous, the holes made by it should be prominent. The stitch is worked round all the design lines through both layers of fabric, taking care not to carry the thread from one shape to another. Start by leaving an end of thread which can be darned into the back of the stitches later, and finish by darning into the back of the stitches. Use a No. 24 tapestry needle which acts as a small stiletto, pushing holes in the fabric. Make sure your stitching is accurate first time, and pull the thread tightly enough to emphasise the holes without distorting the fabric.

When the stitching is complete, remove the tacking threads and cut away the excess fabric at the back *as close to the stitches as possible*, taking care *not* to cut the stitches or organdie. Lace scissors are best for this job. Small enclosed spaces, such as the centre of this design, require particular care when starting to cut. When doing this, lift the

Fig. 38 Tack two layers of fabric together, working from the centre, in the direction of the arrows

Fig. 37 Actual-size pattern for shadow appliqué illustrated in Fig. 32

fabric with a needle, make sure it is free of the organdie and snip in the centre of the shape, making a hole just large enough to insert the rounded tip of the scissor blade between the fabric and organdie.

Making up Mark the position of the footside of the lace by tacking. Use the single-layer bias binding method (described on page 36 of *Mounting and Using Lace*) for finishing the edge, cutting the binding from the fabric used for the appliqué. When the binding has been folded over to the wrong side of the mat, stitch it in place all round through both layers of fabric, working from the right side 5 mm ($\frac{3}{16}$ inch) in from the edge using four-sided stitch. Cut away the excess fabric as close to the stitching as possible – this method was chosen because it makes a reasonably strong hem which blends with the lace and embroidery. From the point of view of appearance a direct method seems a good idea but as organdie frays easily the result would not be strong enough to stand much laundering.

Alternatives 1) Different colours could be used in some areas by tacking separate pieces of fabric under some shapes. If these different colours will lie close to each other in the finished design, work as follows – tack and stitch one colour, then cut away excess fabric before tacking the next colour into place.
2) The pricking in Fig. 34a is 1/6th of a circle and could be used to make a complete circle, in which case the embroidery design could be adapted by omitting the section between lines **A–A** and **B–B** in Fig. 37.
3) For a longer runner, the embroidery design can be extended by repeating the section between lines **A–A** and **B–B** in Fig. 37 as many times as required.
4) The prickings in Fig. 34 could be combined as shown in Fig. 36b to make an unusual table centre.

Torchon bookmark

This is a simple Torchon bookmark with a piece of ribbon threaded into it, illustrated in Fig. 39.

Materials   Tanne No. 30 – 14 pairs wound with rose-pink and two pairs (fan weavers) wound with deep pink
Embroidery ribbon, 1.5 mm ($\frac{1}{16}$ inch) wide, in shade to match fan weavers (see list of suppliers)

The lace   Referring to Figs 40, 41a and 41b, start with the cloth stitch section at the top by introducing pairs from temporary pins above as indicated. Work as far as **A** where two pairs are introduced; the outer pair will become the fan weavers. Now work back in cloth stitch through three pairs of passives and set pin **B** between the weavers and the last pair of passives worked through. The right-hand pair of these two, previously passives, now become weavers which work to **C**. Continue working this cloth section in the usual way; there should be two pairs left hanging from pin **A**. Work the opposite side in a similar way.

The fans are worked in whole stitch, twisting as indicated by dashes in Fig. 41b.

The ground stitch used is whole stitch, twist, pin, whole stitch, twist which gives a firm, rather square hole to hold the ribbon securely.

The bookmark finishes with the cloth stitch section at the bottom. Referring to Fig. 41c, work as usual to pin **X** and from there work through four pairs to the right; set pin **Y** between the weavers and the last pair of passives worked through. Close the pin with these pairs and then use the right-hand pair of these two to work across to **Z**. Now continue across to **V**. Leave two pairs (including the fan weavers) hanging from **Z** and one pair from each of the outside pins. Work the opposite side in a similar manner. Tie the fan weavers and lay them to the back of the pillow; later they will be cut off and darned into the fan. They are not included in the tassel because of their colour.

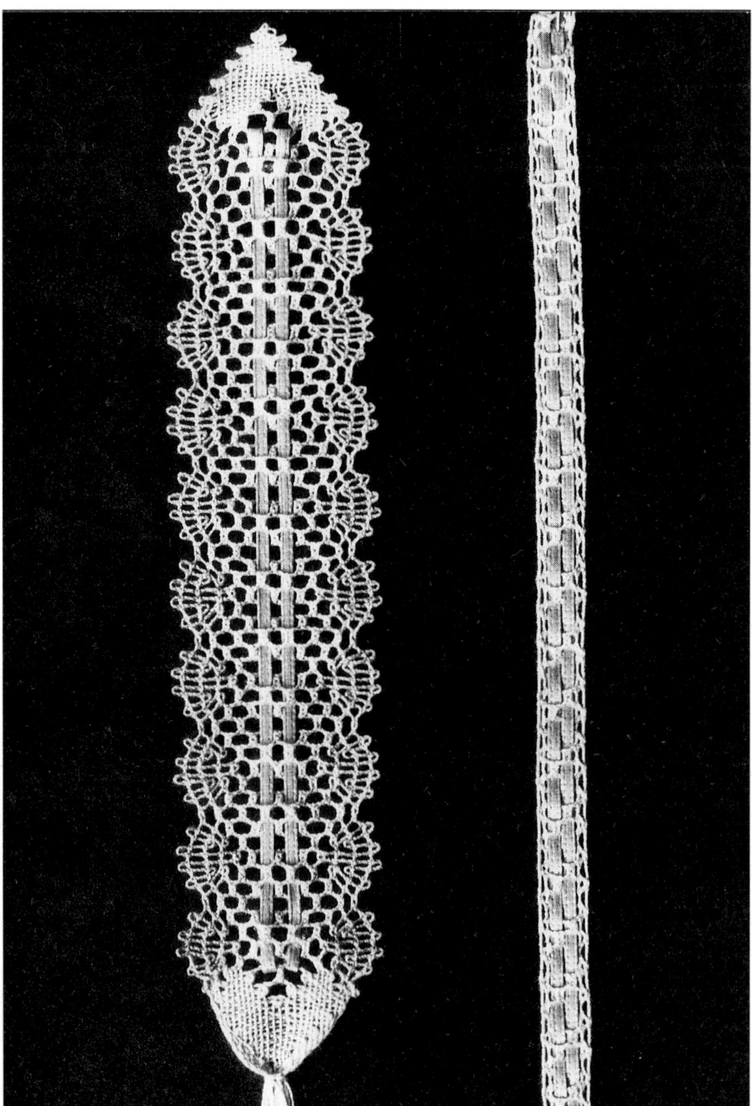

Fig. 39 Torchon bookmark
and braid for the smaller
lampshade illustrated in
Fig. 42

Fig. 40 Pricking for the
bookmark shown in Fig. 39

Work in cloth stitch throughout to make the tassel. Proceed as
follows:
Take the pair from **G** through one pair from **Z** and leave.
Now take the pair from **H** through two pairs on the right and leave.
Now take the pair from **I** through three pairs on the right and leave.
Continue in this way until the right-hand pair from **L** is worked
    through six pairs.
Pull up the pair from **L** firmly, tying in a reef knot.
Do the same with the remaining pairs on this side.

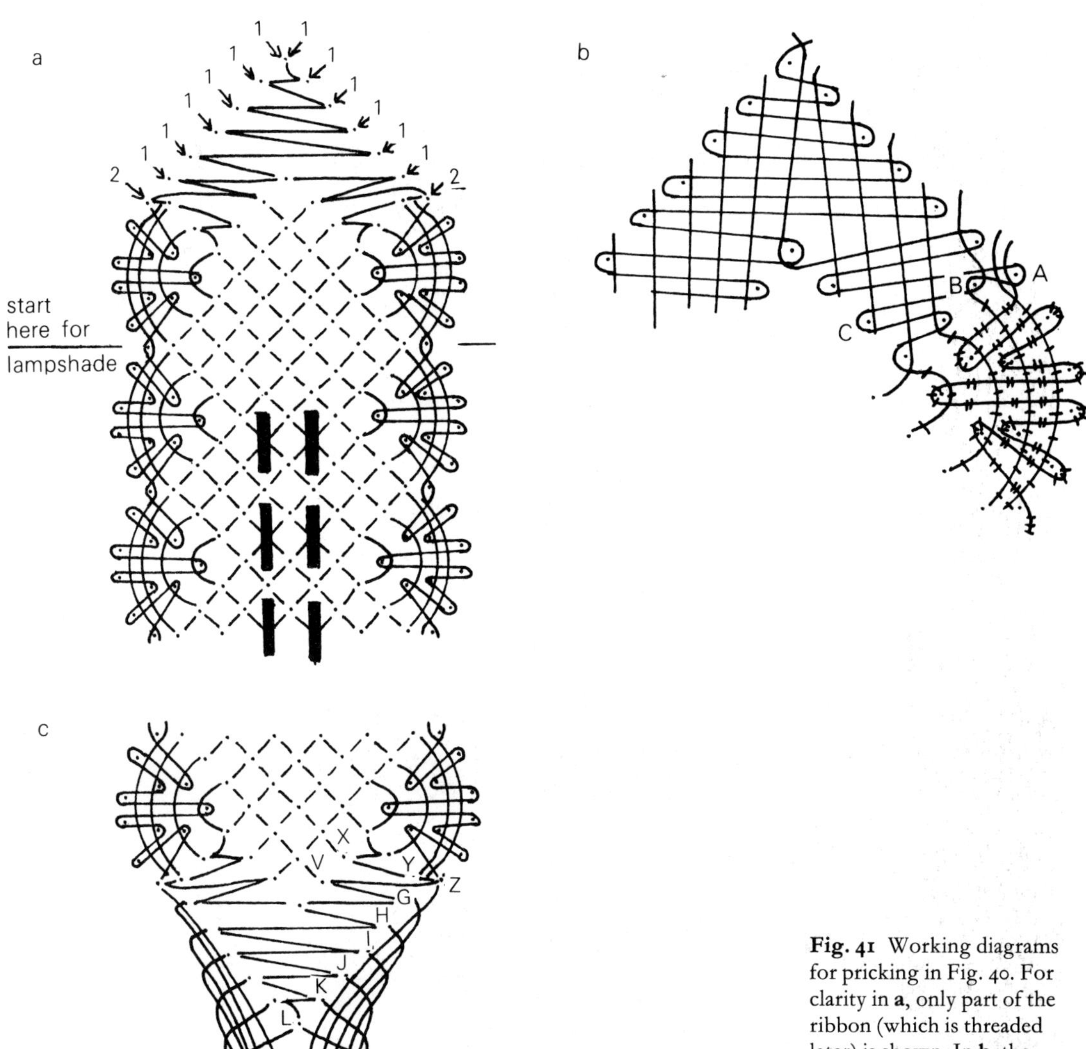

Fig. 41 Working diagrams for pricking in Fig. 40. For clarity in **a**, only part of the ribbon (which is threaded later) is shown. In **b**, the dashes on the lines in the fan indicate the number of times the pairs are twisted

Work the opposite side in a similar way, reading 'left' for 'right'. Finally, lift all pairs except the outside ones (originally from **L**) in a bundle, and cross the outside pairs under it. Put the bundle down and tie one bobbin from each side firmly over it, in a reef knot; then lay this pair with the bundle. The remaining two bobbins are treated in the same way. Cut off to the required length.

Referring to Figs 39 and 41, thread the ribbon through, making sure it is not twisted; a tapestry needle is ideal for this job. Take care with the tension so that lace and ribbon both lie flat. Fold the end of ribbon to the back and catch stitch to itself.

Small lampshade

This lampshade makes use of the bookmark pricking in Fig. 40, and is shown in Fig. 42. Although a small frame was used for the original, the same idea could be adapted for a larger shade. Lace is best used to trim straight, simple frames.

Fig. 42 Two lampshades. The wooden base for the smaller one was made by Malcolm Thorpe

Materials　　Tanne No. 30 – 14 pairs wound with rose-pink and 2 pairs (fan weavers) wound with deep pink

Tanne No. 30 – 7 pairs wound with rose-pink for the braid

Embroidery ribbon, 1.5 mm ($\frac{1}{16}$ inch) wide, in shade to match fan weavers (see list of suppliers)

Piece of fabric, approx. 27 cm (10$\frac{1}{2}$ inches) by 36 cm (14 inches), for lampshade cover

Piece of fabric, approx. 27 cm (10$\frac{1}{2}$ inches) by 36 cm (14 inches), for lampshade lining (for the original, cream satin was used for both)

Lampshade frame, 13 cm (5 inches) diameter at the base and 12 cm (4$\frac{3}{4}$ inches) high, with six straight struts

3 m (3$\frac{1}{4}$ yards approx.) of bias binding

The lace　　If necessary, the pricking should be extended to fit the height of the shade, remembering that the cloth stitch sections at top and bottom will be omitted.

Start along a straight line as indicated in Fig. 41a, and finish along a similar straight line by simply tying each pair in a reef knot and cutting off close to the knot. Make the lace as near to the correct length as possible to avoid bulk. Thread the ribbon and catch its ends in place on the lace without folding back the ends.

Making the braid　　This should be made after covering and lining the lampshade. Refer to Figs 39, 43 and 44. Torchon edge stitch is worked on each side, and the ground stitch is the same as for the bookmark. Measure accurately round the outside of the frame after its lining has been stitched in place (see below). Check that you work complete pattern repeats to ensure the even threading of the ribbon. Join the braid into a circle on the pillow, checking that it is not twisted. The ends of thread can be tucked under the braid when stitching it to the frame. Thread one length of ribbon but do not fasten it off; the lace can be eased to size, but the ribbon cannot. Now pin the braid into place, taking care not to catch the ribbon in with the pins, and adjust the ribbon to fit by overlapping the ends. The ends of the ribbon are now pinned together before removing the braid from the frame. They are then stitched together and the ribbon eased round so that the cut end is hidden under a ground stitch. Insert the second ribbon in the same way.

Making the lampshade　　Make sure the frame is smooth and, if it is not plastic covered, paint it to prevent rust.

Bind the frame with either tape or bias binding. If using bias binding (which I did) open out and press flat one of the seam allowances. The binding colour can be chosen to suit the fabric – I used white.

Start binding the struts by folding the tape over the top ring and wrapping the binding over its folded end (see Fig. 45a). Bind tightly and evenly to keep the fabric smooth and avoid excess bulk. At the bottom, take the binding over the lower ring and then bring it back

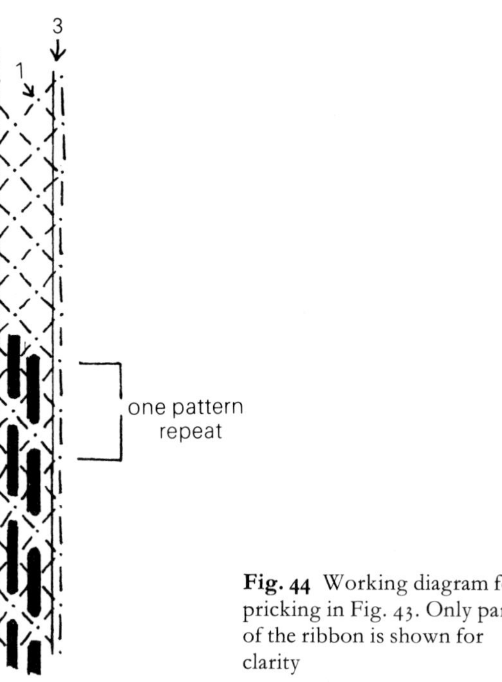

Fig. 44 Working diagram for pricking in Fig. 43. Only part of the ribbon is shown for clarity

Fig. 43 Pricking for the braid illustrated in Fig. 39

to lie along the strut. Stitch it firmly in place and cut the end off neatly.

Bind all the struts in this way but do *not* finish off the tape on the last one. Instead, make a figure of eight round the bottom ring and then continue to bind the lower ring, making a figure of eight round each strut in turn. Finish off in a similar way to the struts.

Bind the top ring, starting and finishing in a similar way to the struts; remember to make a figure of eight round each strut.

The cover is prepared by folding the fabric in half, right sides together, and pinning the two layers together. Referring to Fig. 45b, pin the fabric onto half of the frame, starting with pins at **A**, **B**, **C** and **D** and with the straight grain running down the centre. The pins should go into the binding towards the outside of the frame, *not* round struts. Pin along the struts at intervals of 2.5 cm (1 inch) and then round the rings at the same intervals, making sure that the fabric is pulled tightly and evenly. Gradually insert pins until they are about 6 mm ($\frac{1}{4}$ inch) apart all around.

When the fabric is pinned satisfactorily, mark the position of struts **A–C** and **B–D** by drawing lightly over them on the fabric with a sharp, hard pencil; also mark the position of the top and bottom rings along this line. Remove the fabric from the frame and machine along the marked lines, stretching the fabric slightly as you stitch and extending the stitching 1.2 cm ($\frac{1}{2}$ inch) beyond the position of the rings.

Now prepare the lining in exactly the same way but machine about 3 mm ($\frac{1}{8}$ inch) in from the marked lines, and place on one side until required.

To fit the cover, trim the side seams only, to about 6 mm ($\frac{1}{4}$ inch), and press to one side (do *not* press open). Turn the cover to the right side and pull on to the frame, keeping the seams straight and in line with two struts. Now pin to the top and bottom rings as before, making sure the fabric is smooth and tight.

The cover may now be stitched into place, using a double, matching sewing thread. Overcast the fabric to the binding, keeping the stitching close and even and well to the top and bottom of the frame respectively. Finally, cut away the excess fabric, close to the stitching.

a

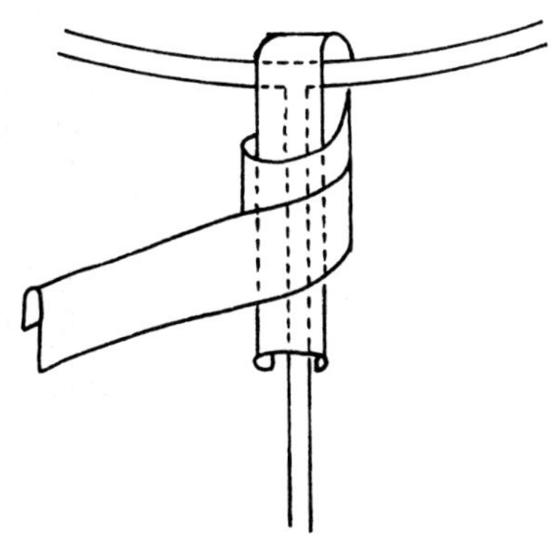

Fig. 45 Covering a lampshade:
a Starting the binding
b Pinning fabric in place
c Neatening the fitting

b

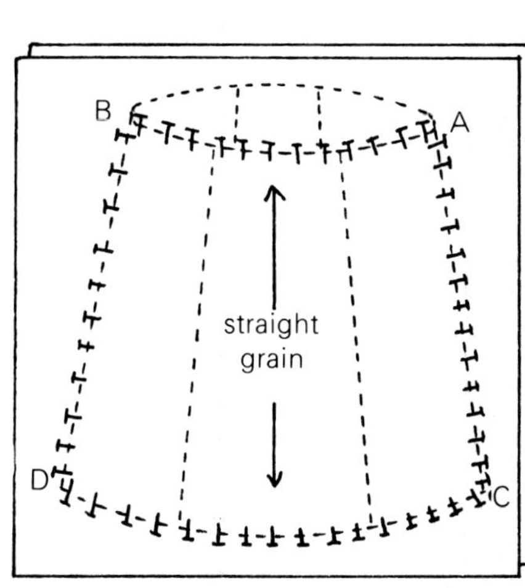

c

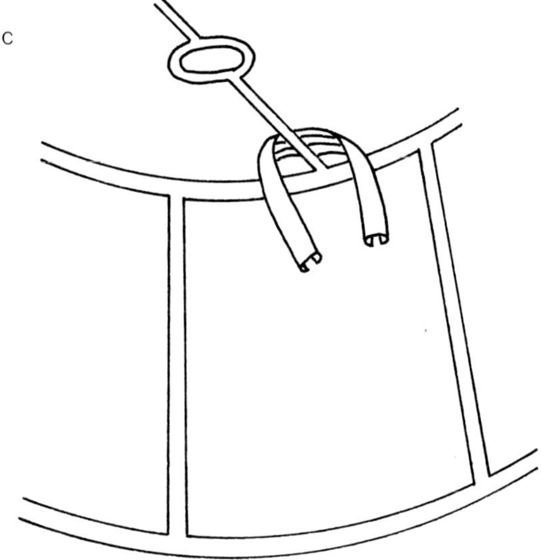

Now pin the lace into place, keeping each strip placed centrally over each strut. Oversew the ends in place over the stitching that holds the cover. Invisibly sew both edges of each strip into place, making sure that there are no long threads at the back which will show when the shade is lit. Work with a stab stitch, with your 'best' hand inside the frame as if you were working with an embroidery frame (this is easier on a large frame but awkward on a small one). Alternatively, work from the outside using a fine curved needle.

When all the lace is in place, check that there are no loose threads inside before fitting the lining inside the frame. Again, line up the seams with the struts and pin to the top and bottom rings, pulling the fabric so that it is tight and even. If the top fitting is in line with the seams, open the seams to allow the fabric to fit round it. If not, the fabric must be slit very carefully so that it will lie smooth but not leave a gap under the fitting. The lining may now be stitched into place in the same way as the cover, keeping the stitches well to the front of the frame, where they will be covered by the braid. Again, cut the excess fabric away, close to the stitching.

It is now necessary to neaten round the fitting. Do this by cutting a bias strip of lining fabric approximately 2.5 cm (1 inch) by 8.5 cm ($3\frac{1}{4}$ inches) and then press under 6 mm ($\frac{1}{4}$ inch) along both long edges to make a strip approximately 1.2 cm ($\frac{1}{2}$ inch) wide. Place it under the fitting as shown in Fig. 45c, pinning it to the outside of the frame and making sure it is pulled up tight with no raw edges showing round the fitting. Then stitch it to the outside of the frame in the same way as the lining; the excess length is then cut off close to the stitching.

Finally, make the braid for the top and bottom as described on page 49 and pin it to the shade, covering all the raw edges and the stitching. Hem stitch neatly in place along both edges, tucking in the ends of thread and making sure that no stitching goes through to the lining (slide the needle along between cover and lining).

1) Applied down the sleeve or across the yoke of a blouse or dress.
2) Strips applied across a cushion.
3) For a bridal head-dress – see page 65. It may look particularly attractive if metallic threads are used for the weavers.
4) On an epaulette for a blouse or dress – see Fig. 93.

Lampshade

This lampshade has a strip of matching lace inserted down the centre of each panel of the cover. The struts are covered with an applied strip of lace in a colour to match the lining fabric. The pricking in Fig. 47 may be used for a bookmark, and Figs 46 and 48 illustrate the beginning and end when used for this. For the lampshade, start and finish along a straight line which will be covered by the lining.

The lampshade is illustrated in Fig. 42.

Materials Straight-sided frame, 16 cm (6¼ inches) high and 23 cm (9 inches) diameter at the base, with four struts

Approx. 2.8 m (3 yards) of bias binding

Cotton fabric for cover – approx. 50 cm (19¾ inches) square (the original was pink)

Cotton fabric for lining, in contrasting colour, approx. 50 cm (19¾ inches) square (the original was yellow)

Insertion
– 32 pairs Tanne No. 50 (to match cover fabric – the original used rose-pink)
– 1 pair and two single gimp bobbins Coton à Broder No. 25 (the original used a deeper pink)

Applied strip
– 28 pairs Brilliante d'Alsace No. 50
– 2 pairs gimp bobbins Coton à Broder No. 25 (both yellow to match lining)

Braid
– Two pairs Perle No. 8 (yellow)
– Nine pairs Tanne No. 30 (pink to match lace)

Fringe
– Two pairs Perle No. 8 (yellow)
– One pair Perle No. 8 (pink to match lace – largest possible bobbins). One ball was sufficient for this size of shade
– Eight pairs Tanne No. 30 (pink to match lace)

The lace The lace should be made as near to the exact length as possible, to avoid excessive bulk, and may be started and finished along a straight line. To finish, each pair of threads may be tied in a reef knot and cut off close to the knot. Refer to Figs 47 and 48 for pricking and working diagram for the applied strip, and Figs 49 and 50 for the

Fig. 46 Detail of lace on the larger lampshade illustrated in Fig. 42

insertion. Two variations for working the same pricking are illustrated – only the gimp lines are different, *not* the pinholes. Either or both may be used, but it is preferable to work version **A** for the applied strips because the more solid centre gives a better covering for the struts and stitching; the more open version **B** was used for the insertion, for contrast. These prickings show the gimp lines as they were used to make the lace illustrated in Fig. 46; if you intend to work the variation, they must be redrawn referring to Figs 48 and 50.

Making the braid

The braid is best made after the shade has been covered and lined. Referring to Figs 51, 52 and 53a, hang pairs as indicated. The braid is worked in whole stitch with an edge stitch on each side; the edge stitch is worked in whole stitch and three twists. To work the two yellow Perle pairs in the centre, work in cloth stitch through the three pairs of pink passives and then pass the weavers *between* one pair of Perle thread. Twist the Perle pair once, work the next pair in the same way and then work through three pairs of pink passives in

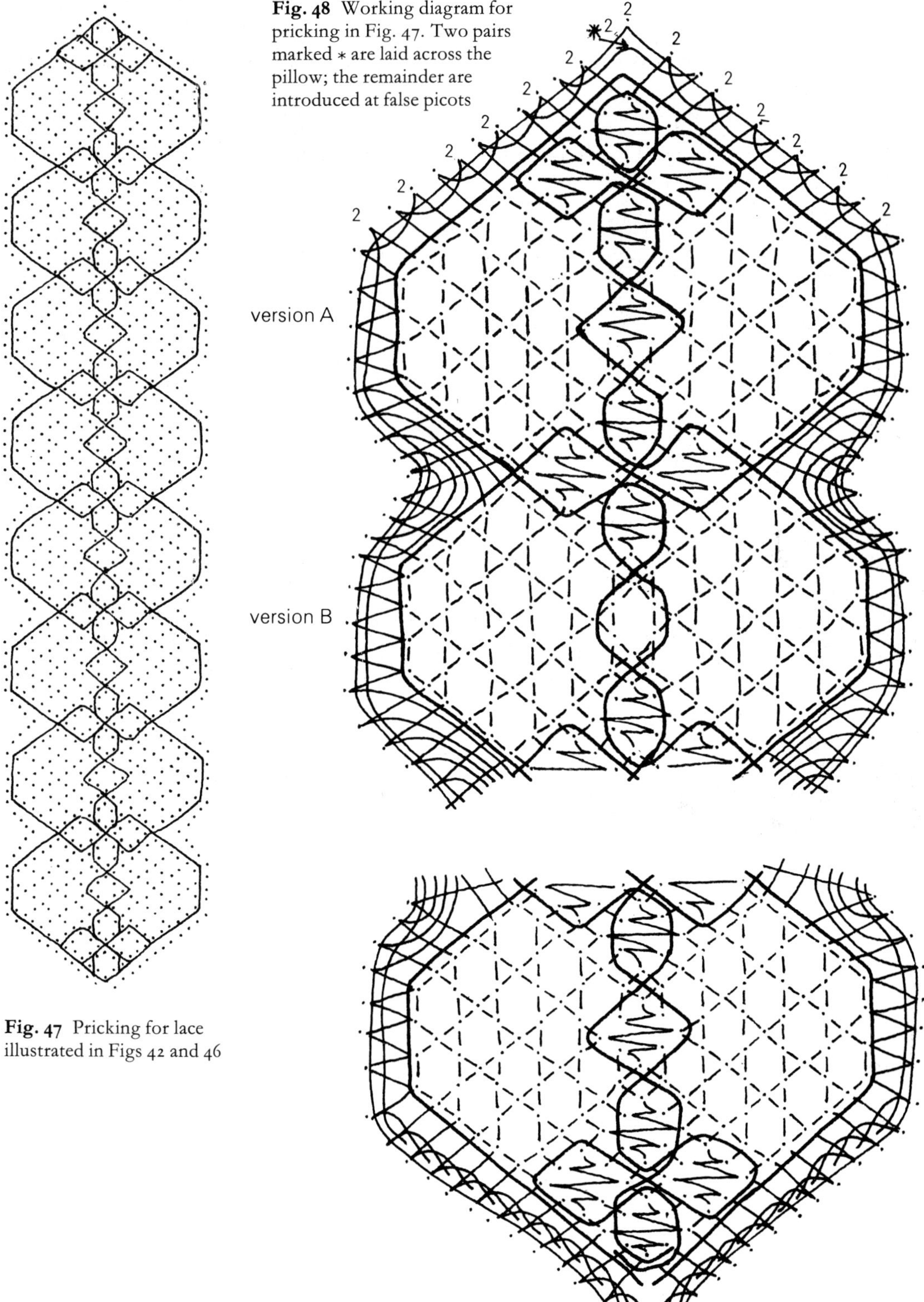

Fig. 48 Working diagram for pricking in Fig. 47. Two pairs marked * are laid across the pillow; the remainder are introduced at false picots

Fig. 47 Pricking for lace illustrated in Figs 42 and 46

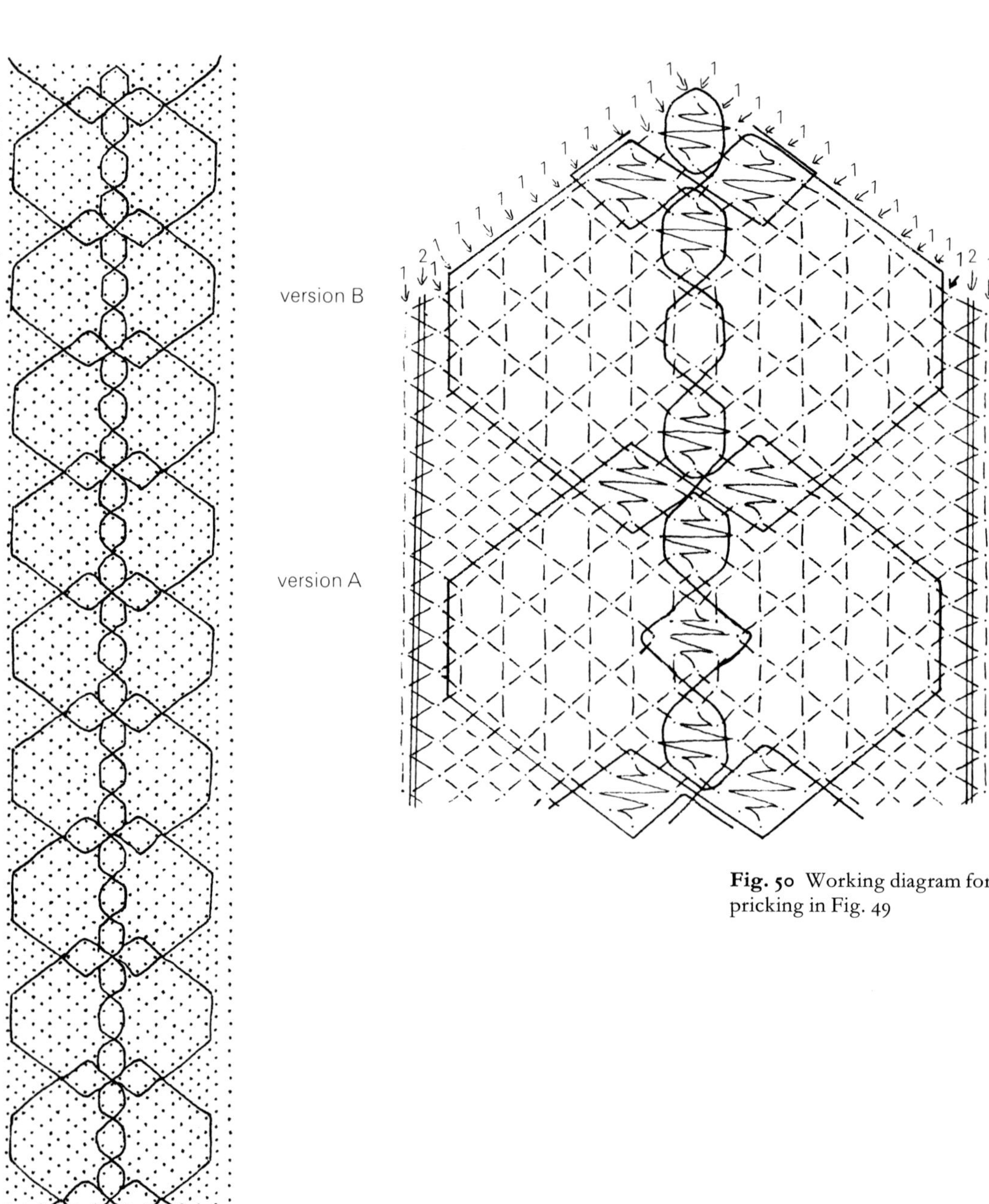

Fig. 50 Working diagram for
pricking in Fig. 49

Fig. 49 Pricking for lace
insertion in Figs 42 and 46

Fig. 51 Detail of braid and fringe used for larger lampshade illustrated in Fig. 42

cloth stitch (see Fig. 53c). Note that the Perle pairs do *not* make a stitch. Work all rows in the same way. To finish, tie each pair in a reef knot before cutting off. These ends can be tucked under the braid when it is stitched into place on the frame.

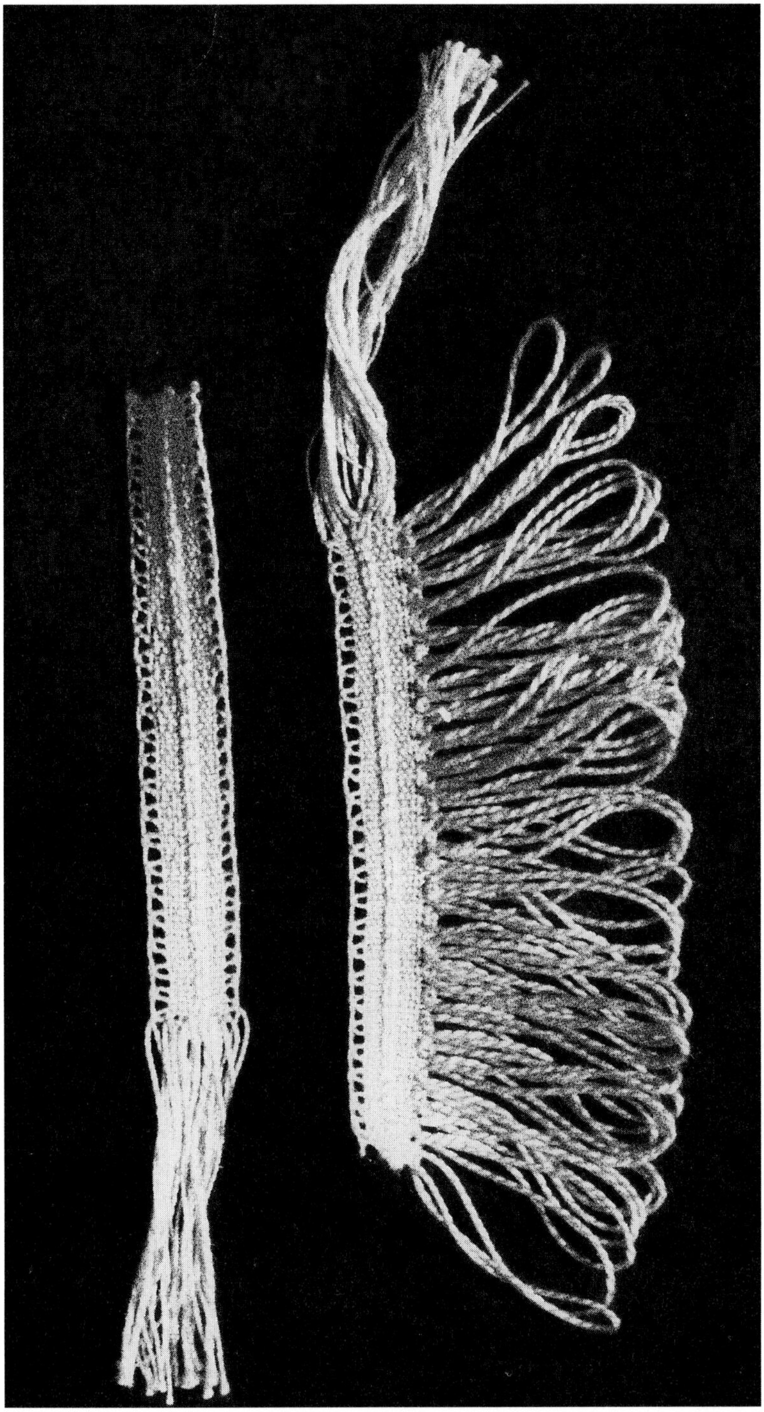

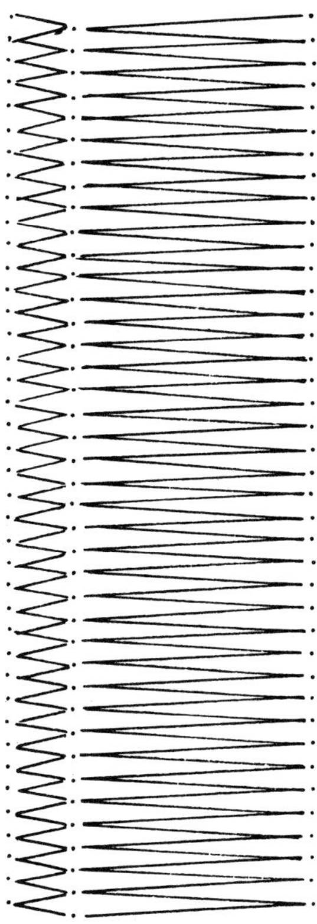

Fig. 52 Pricking for braid and fringe illustrated in Fig. 51. For the braid, omit the row of pinholes on the right-hand side

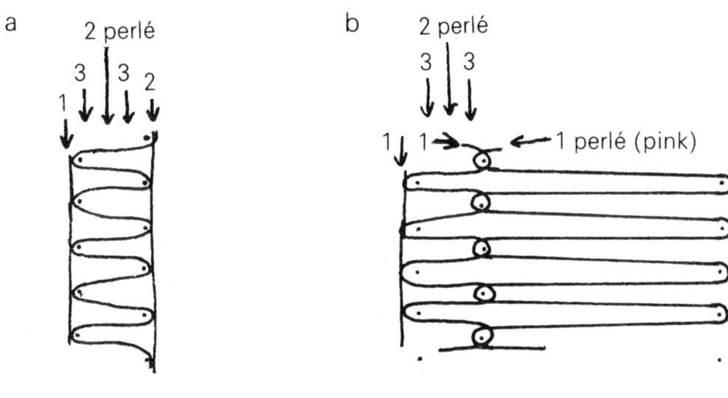

Fig. 53
a Working diagram for braid
b Working diagram for fringe
c Method of working two
Perle pairs in braid and
fringe. Each line represents
one thread.

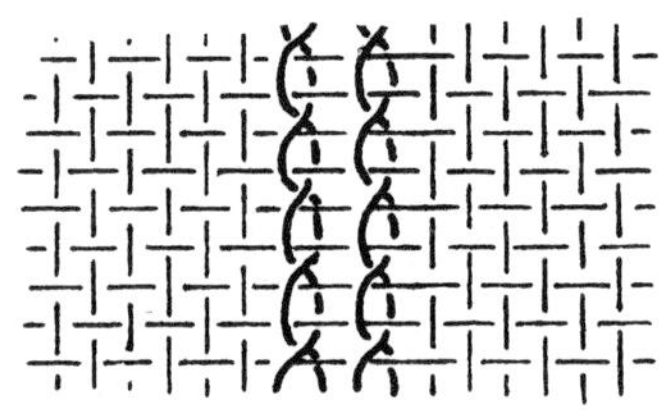

Making the fringe

The fringe is best made after covering and lining the frame. Referring to Figs 51, 52 and 53b, hang pairs as indicated. The left-hand edge stitch and all passive pairs are worked in the same way as for the braid. Work the centre pin with the pair of pink Perle and a pair of Tanne No. 30 (the weavers) as follows: whole stitch, twist both pairs once, set the centre pin between them and close the pin with a whole stitch (*no* twists). The Perle pair for the fringe travels round the next pin on the right-hand side and comes back to work the next centre pin with the weavers, which are returning from an edge stitch on the left-hand side. When it is necessary to join in a new Perle thread for the fringe, work the centre pin as above and then make a weaver's knot right against the pin. The ends can be tucked under the braid on the lampshade.

Making the lampshade

Prepare and bind the frame and then prepare the lining as for the small lampshade (see page 49). The outer cover, however, is constructed differently so that the grain of the fabric will run down the centre of each panel.

Cut a piece of fabric large enough for *one* panel and insert the lace in the centre, making sure that the grain is straight. As a hem would be too heavy when lit, use a direct method (three-sided stitch is the strongest). Withdraw a thread if you like, to keep the stitching even, and use the same thread as to make the lace. Now cut away the excess fabric at the back before pinning on to the frame. Pin it into place (as on the small shade) all round, pulling the fabric taut and making sure that the lace is straight and central on the panel. When satisfied, stitch it into place all round, keeping the stitching well to the top or bottom of the rings and well over the side struts. Cut off the excess fabric close to the stitching all round. Add the next section (with lace inserted) in the same way. On the side struts the fabric will cover the previous line of stitching. Continue until all the panels are in place.

Now apply lace over each strut, making sure that it is central. Stitch it invisibly into place using a stabbing movement as if working in an embroidery frame. When all the lace is in place, check that there are no loose threads inside and then line the frame in the same way as for the small shade.

Finally, stitch the braid into place on the top edge and the fringe on the lower edge, making sure no stitches show through on the lining. The fringe may be left as it is (as illustrated in Fig. 51) or the loops may be cut, as shown in Fig. 42.

Alternatives These prickings can be used in a variety of ways; the following are some suggestions:

1) The pricking in Fig. 47 can be used as a bookmark as described above, the top and bottom of which are illustrated in Fig. 46.

2) Either pricking could be used to make a bridal head-dress (see page 65); note that the pricking used for the jabot on page 74 matches these prickings and could be used to trim the veil and also the dress.

3) The pricking in Fig. 49 could be used in the sleeve or on the front of a blouse or dress.

Handkerchief

Fig. 54 Handkerchief

This edging is attached to a bought handkerchief but, because it is almost always impossible to make the lace the exact size, buying a handkerchief should be considered as a convenient way of buying a small amount of fabric. The original handkerchief was yellow with a woven white stripe pattern, so the lace was made in exactly matching yellow thread with a white gimp. After the lace was finished, I cut off the existing hem and made a double fold hem 5 mm ($\frac{3}{16}$ inch) deep with mitred corners, pin-stitched into place, making sure that it exactly followed the straight grain. If there is insufficient fabric for a hem, then one of the direct methods must be used.

The finished size of the handkerchief, including lace, is approx. 27.5 cm ($10\frac{3}{4}$ inches) square. It is illustrated in Fig. 54, and a detail of the lace is shown in Fig. 55.

Fig. 55 Detail of handkerchief shown in Fig. 54. Shows join in lace from the wrong side

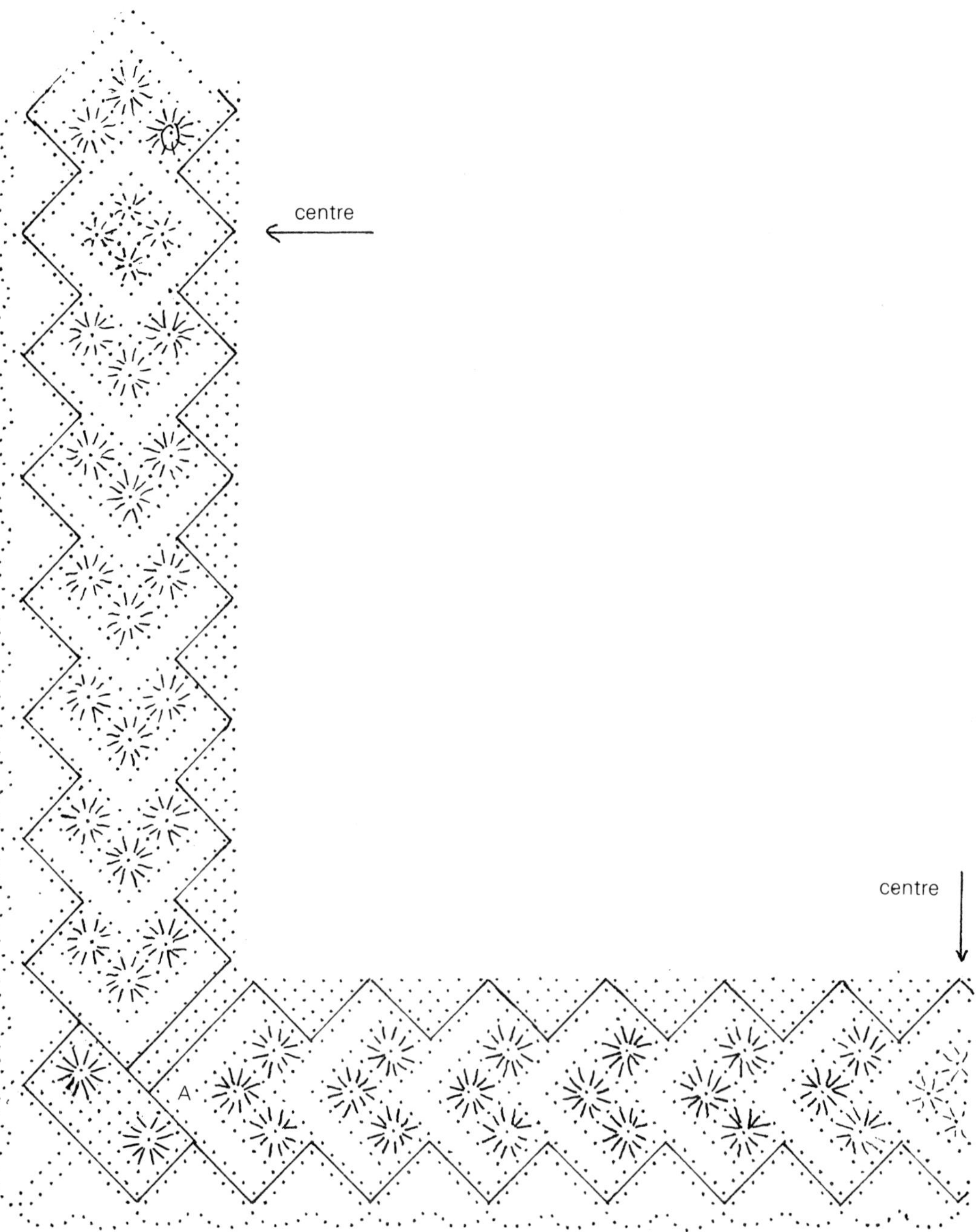

Fig. 56 Pricking for lace
illustrated in Figs 54 and 55

Fig. 57 Working diagrams
for pricking in Fig. 56:
a To start
b Centre reversal
c Corner showing gimps
finished off

Materials	Brilliante d'Alsace No. 50 – 26 pairs
	Perle No. 8 – 3 single gimp bobbins

The lace When preparing the pricking, note that there is a centre pattern reversal and its appearance will be improved if the weavers are changed for the second half of the half stitch (see note 2 on page 11). Before starting, you should also note that the gimp is not introduced in the most obvious place; read the instructions below carefully. The gimp is started in the way described so that it will travel through all four corners of the lace in the same way and be fastened securely at the end.

Referring to Figs 56 and 57a, start with the corner chevron of half stitch (**A**) by hanging pairs from temporary pins and working as indicated. Do not introduce the gimp. Now work the three spiders, and then introduce a single gimp bobbin on the right-hand side as indicated in Fig. 57a. Leave a long end of gimp thread, at least 20 cm (8 inches) behind your work (this will later need to be wound on to a bobbin). Now work the footside edge and the triangle of ground.

Next introduce the second single gimp thread as indicated in Fig. 57a, again leaving a long end behind your work. The cloth stitch fan may then be started using two pairs and a single gimp. Remember to work the edge passives in whole stitch and twist, and also to twist the weavers before and after passing the gimp through them. The working should now be straightforward. Refer to Fig. 57b for the centre reversal.

To complete the lace, refer to Fig. 57c. Work the last row of ground stitches on the right-hand side and then pass the gimp through the pairs as usual. Now wind the loose end of the gimp left at the beginning on the foot side on to a bobbin and pass it back through the same pairs to the top of the chevron. Both of these gimp threads are laid back to be cut off later.

When the last fan **X** has been worked, bring the gimp thread through all pairs from the fan as usual. The loose end left at the beginning is then wound on to a bobbin and passed back through the same pairs. Lay both gimps back to be cut off later, sew in and tie all the pairs and cut off all the bobbins.

To finish the ends of the threads, the single gimp threads on the fan edge are overcast to the back of the gimp and the remaining gimps cut off close to the lace. The two pairs on the footside may be darned away into the hem of the fabric. The two pairs from the fan can be darned into the fan. All the remaining pairs can be formed into rolls and overcast to the back of the gimp.

Alternatives 1) This pattern would be very suitable for a veil edging, but remember to lengthen the pricking between the corner and centre reversal.

2) The gimp could be omitted (it is illustrated worked in this way on page 41 of *Mounting and Using Lace*) but it is almost impossible to make an invisible join without it.

Clutch bag and handkerchief
with lace corner

Mat with counted-thread
embroidery

Oval mat with shadow
appliqué

Bridal head-dress

Other prickings and styles of lace are equally suitable for use in this manner, which enables a delicate lace to be used with no problem about it keeping its shape when worn, especially on a wet and windy day. The original was white lace mounted on gold lamé. The head-dress is illustrated in Fig. 58, and a detail of the lace is shown in Fig. 59.

Fig. 58 Bridal head-dress

Fig. 59 Detail of lace shown in Fig. 58

Materials	Tanne No. 50 – 32 pairs
	Belt backing (buckram-type) 5 cm (2 inches) wide – approx. 0.5 m ($\frac{1}{2}$ yard)
	Pearl embroidery beads 2.5 mm in diameter
	Gold lamé (or satin, or other suitable) fabric 44 cm (17$\frac{1}{4}$ inches) by 16 cm (6$\frac{1}{4}$ inches)

The lace The lace for the original was about 42 cm (16$\frac{1}{2}$ inches) long, but the size may be adjusted to suit the hairstyle. To work, refer to Figs 60 and 61, noting that the centre tallies are leaf-shaped, and those in the edge have square ends. Join into a circle on the pillow (put in pins, pushing them right down where the first pinholes of lace will be to prevent working too far). Work up to these pins, then pin back the start of the lace and join, taking care that the lace is not twisted. The ends of thread need not be darned into the lace.

Making up After removing the lace from the pillow, measure its length accurately. Cut a strip of the fabric of this length plus seam allowances, 8 cm (3$\frac{1}{4}$ inches) wide. Seam the short ends together and press open.

Cut the belt backing to the length of the fabric plus a 1.5 cm ($\frac{5}{8}$ inch) overlap, then lap the ends flat and stitch. Slip the fabric and lace into place over the buckram; check that both lie smoothly; if not, adjust the length of the fabric and/or belt backing as required. Remove the backing and stitch the lace invisibly into place along both edges, all round, checking that it is in the centre of the fabric. Use a fine needle to avoid marking, and thread the ends of the lace to the back of the fabric.

Stitch a tiny pearl bead to the centre of each 'flower', taking the stitch right through the fabric. This prevents the bead from pulling the lace out of shape.

The fabric may now be put back on to the belt backing and the edges folded to the inside – they can be held temporarily in place with sticky tape at intervals, which is preferable with fabrics which are liable to be marked by pinning. Lace the edges together at the back (alternatively, you may do this *before* stitching the lace into place. It is easier to place the lace accurately this way, but is harder work to stitch).

Now prepare the lining from the same fabric, making it about 3 mm ($\frac{1}{8}$ inch) shorter than the outer fabric. Make the short seam, press it open and then fold the long edges under to make a strip the exact width of the belt backing. Fit it into place (either by pinning or with sticky tape) making sure it is smooth all round. Ladder stitch it into place along the top and bottom edges as neatly as possible; these edges may be covered with a matching couched thread, if required, for neatness.

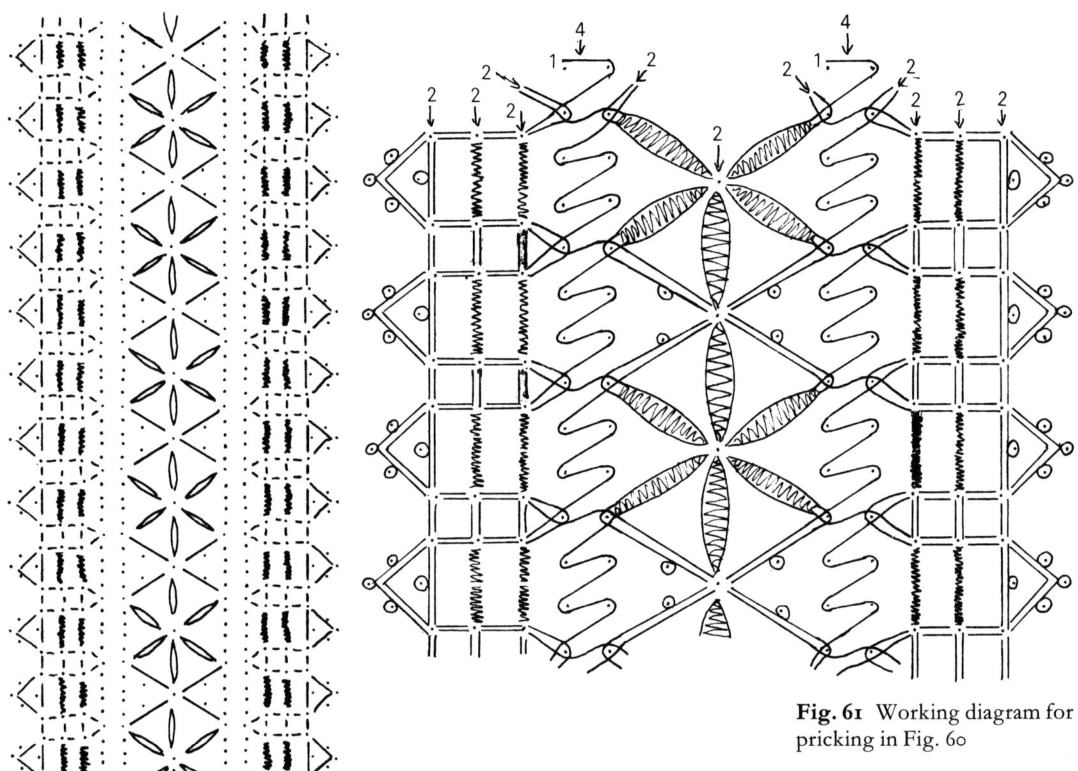

Fig. 61 Working diagram for pricking in Fig. 60

Fig. 60 Pricking for lace illustrated in Figs 58 and 59

Alternatives   This lace could be used in a variety of ways, such as:
1) Applied down the centre line of a sleeve, possibly on the wedding dress itself, or any other blouse or dress (see Fig. 100a).
2) Applied down the centre of a blouse where a concealed button band has been used.
3) For a wedding garter, seam together two lengths of ribbon 2 cm ($\frac{3}{4}$ inch) wide to form a casing for the elastic and then stitch the lace into place so that the outer edges of the cloth stitch trails just cover the ribbon.
4) Applied to a cushion cover, where it could be worked in a thicker thread on an enlarged pricking if you prefer. In this case, either omit the beads or replace them with French knots.
5) Omit the tallies and plaits on one side to make a matching edging.

Other laces could be used in this way:
1) The prickings from the large lampshade (Figs 47 and 49) would be suitable and could be used on a narrower belt backing. The prickings in Fig. 68 match this lace and could be used to edge the veil.
2) The lace on the small lampshade (see page 48) would be suitable; it would be worth trying a metallic thread for the weavers and replacing the ribbon with a heavier metallic thread.
3) For the bridesmaid, the same lace as used on the bride's head-dress could be mounted on a fabric to match her dress, or it could be made in the same colour as her dress and mounted on fabric from the bride's dress.
4) Beds/Maltese-type or Honiton-type motifs could be arranged round the band.
5) The same method could be used (with a narrower belt backing) for a serviette ring. Joining such a short strip of lace on the pillow would be difficult, however, so one or more motifs would be more suitable.

Handkerchief corner or jabot

This pricking is given in two sizes. The larger one was used for the jabot, but the smaller makes a very elegant handkerchief. The jabot illustrated was made in a pale-peach coloured cotton thread and fabric to match the lace on the blouse illustrated in Fig. 96.

Fig. 62 shows the lace on the handkerchief in detail, and the jabot is illustrated in Fig. 96.

Fig. 62 Handkerchief corner

<table>
<tr><td>Materials</td><td>

For the larger pricking:
Tanne No. 50 – 42 pairs
Coton à Broder No. 25 – 4 pairs gimp (this was used for the original but Coton à Broder No. 16 would give a more prominent gimp)
For the smaller pricking:
Tanne No. 80 – 42 pairs
Perle No. 12 – 4 pairs gimp
For the jabot – cotton lawn to match lace – approx. 30 cm (12 inches) by 16 cm (6¼ inches)

</td></tr>
</table>

The lace

To work the lace refer to Figs 63 and 64. All the pairs are introduced from false picots, except the two on the footside and the four pairs which are laid across the pillow, the two right-hand pairs becoming passives on the footside and the two left-hand pairs working on the picot edge.

At the side of those cloth buds marked with an **X**, pass the gimp through the weavers, twist the weavers once and pass the gimp back through them. Continue in the usual way, taking great care with the tension. At the side of those honeycomb buds marked with an **X**, pass the gimp through the adjacent pair from the bud, twist them once then pass the gimp back through, and continue.

As the lace narrows, pairs are laid back from the headside passives as indicated in Fig. 64, and then cut off close to the lace. The few remaining pairs at the end are each tied in a reef knot. These ends may then be darned into the completed hem later.

Making up the handkerchief

Prepare and tack a narrow double-fold hem all round a square handkerchief, remembering to mitre the corners. If you mitre all four corners, you will be able to select the best three. Place the lace into the required position and then mark, by tacking, the position of the footside edge. Remove the lace, fold the handkerchief along this line and prepare a double-fold hem of the same depth as that already prepared, cutting away the excess fabric and taking care not to stretch the fabric. Stitch the hem into place all round the handkerchief using pin stitch, and then flat overcast the lace into place, darning the ends of thread away into the hem.

Making up the jabot

Measure the footside edge of the lace and then cut a piece of fabric twice this width plus seam allowances – 27 cm (10⅝ inches) on the original – by 16 cm (6¼ inches). Fold it in half as shown in Fig. 65, right sides together, and then stitch the seam as indicated by the broken line – 1 cm (⅜ inch) seams are allowed. Clip the corners and seam allowances, turn through to the right side and press. Gather the top (raw) edges to measure 2 cm (¾ inch) and then finish with a matching binding as described on page 93, but using a straight binding.

The lace is then flat overcast into place on the lower edge and the remaining ends of thread are darned into the fabric. The jabot may be pinned into place with a suitable brooch (as illustrated in Fig. 96), or a safety-pin may be stitched to the back of the binding and a small ribbon bow to the front.

Alternatives 1) Four corners could be used on one handkerchief.
2) One corner could be used on each end of a wide tie, which could be tied in a soft bow or a knot.
3) More than one layer could be used for a jabot, with each layer shorter than the next in order to show all the lace.

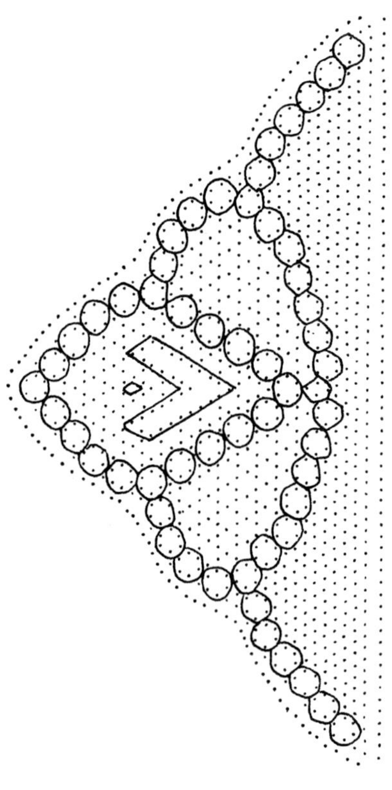

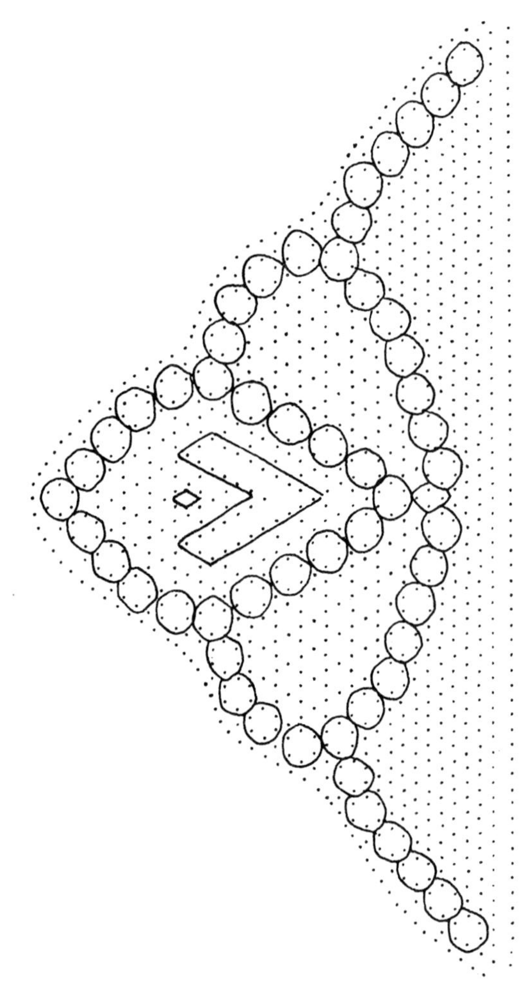

Fig. 63 Pricking (in two sizes) for lace illustrated in Fig. 62

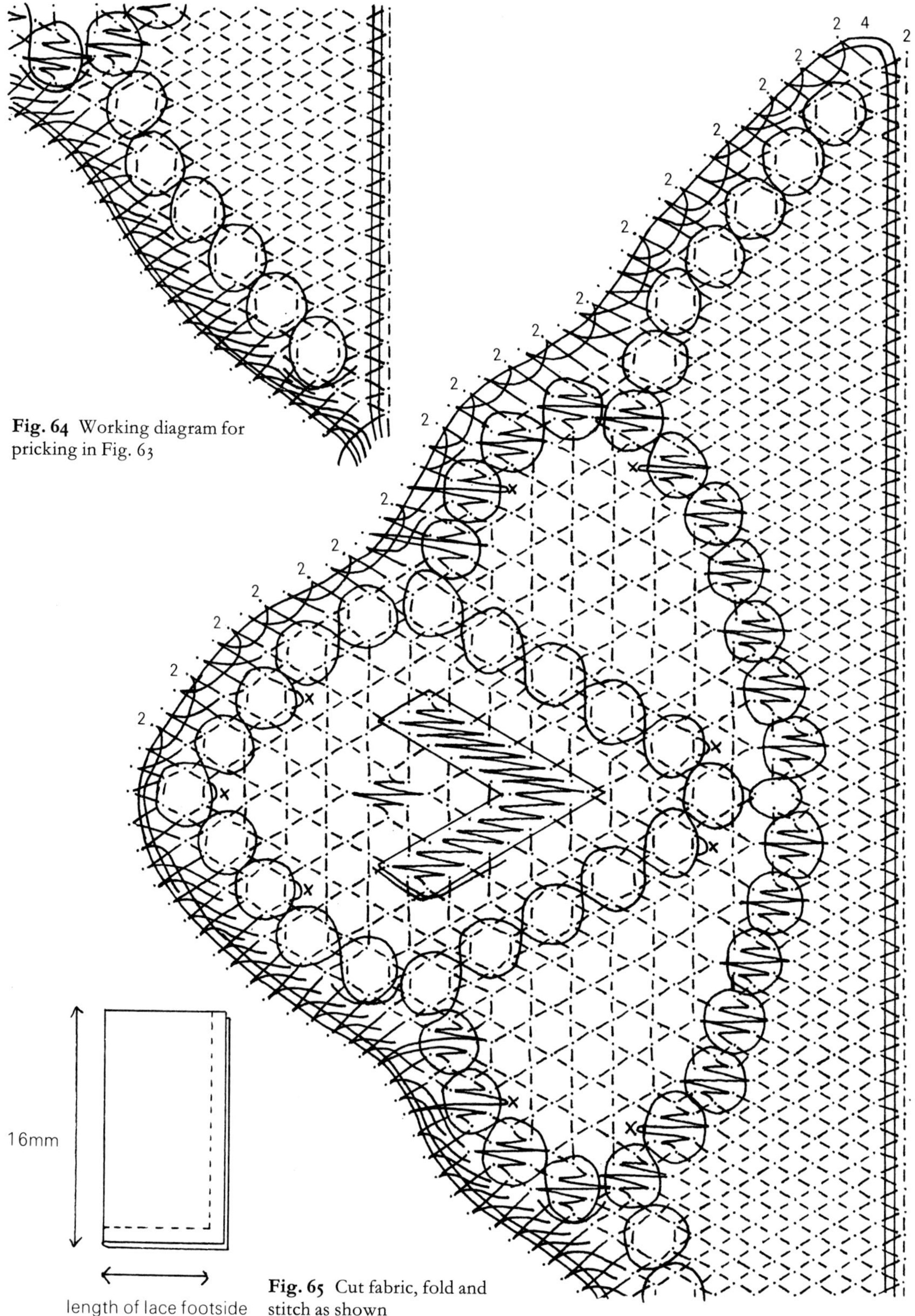

Fig. 64 Working diagram for pricking in Fig. 63

16mm

length of lace footside

Fig. 65 Cut fabric, fold and stitch as shown

Jabot

This is an ideal way of using sample corners – a different one can be used on each layer as long as the designs are similar. Other types of lace, such as fine Torchon or Beds/Maltese, could equally well be used. For a richer effect, more layers could be used, or one layer could be used alone. The hem is shaped to echo the edge of the lace, but it could of course be a simple straight hem. The original was made in white, but a colour to complement the rest of your outfit could be chosen.

The jabot is illustrated in Fig. 66, and a detail of the lace and hem is shown in Fig. 67.

Materials Tanne No. 50 – 26 pairs plus 6 extra pairs for the corner
Perle No. 12 – 1 pair plus 1 single bobbin for the gimp
Matching cotton or linen lawn 24 cm (9½ inches) by 46 cm (18 inches)

The lace Two variations of the same pricking are illustrated in Fig. 68; the pinholes are the same, but the gimp lines and tallies are different. Either or both may be used (this also applies to both laces on the large lampshade); the method of working the corner is the same on both. Follow the working diagrams in Fig. 69 – on the corner, * is used to indicate where extra pairs are added and **O** to indicate where a pair is taken out.

For the jabot start on a convenient diagonal line as shown in Fig. 69, making sure that the seam line will be across the lace when making up. Both ends of the lace will be included in the seam and hidden at the back, so the lace can end with knotted threads cut off short. If you are making a closed border, such as a handkerchief, start where maximum use can be made of the gimp for hiding the join.

Making up Referring to Fig. 70, trace off both sections (one is drawn with a solid line, the other with a broken line) and join them along the line **A–B** to obtain the pattern. Cut out the fabric using this pattern and noting the position of the straight grain. Prepare a single-fold hem along the lower edge of the jabot, mitring the corner. Stitch along the shaped stitching line shown on the pattern with three-sided stitch (this line can be shaped to echo either the edge or a feature of

Fig. 66 Jabot

Fig. 67 Detail of lace illustrated in Fig. 66. For the photograph, a contrasting coloured fabric was placed under the lace on the upper layer in order to show the lace more clearly

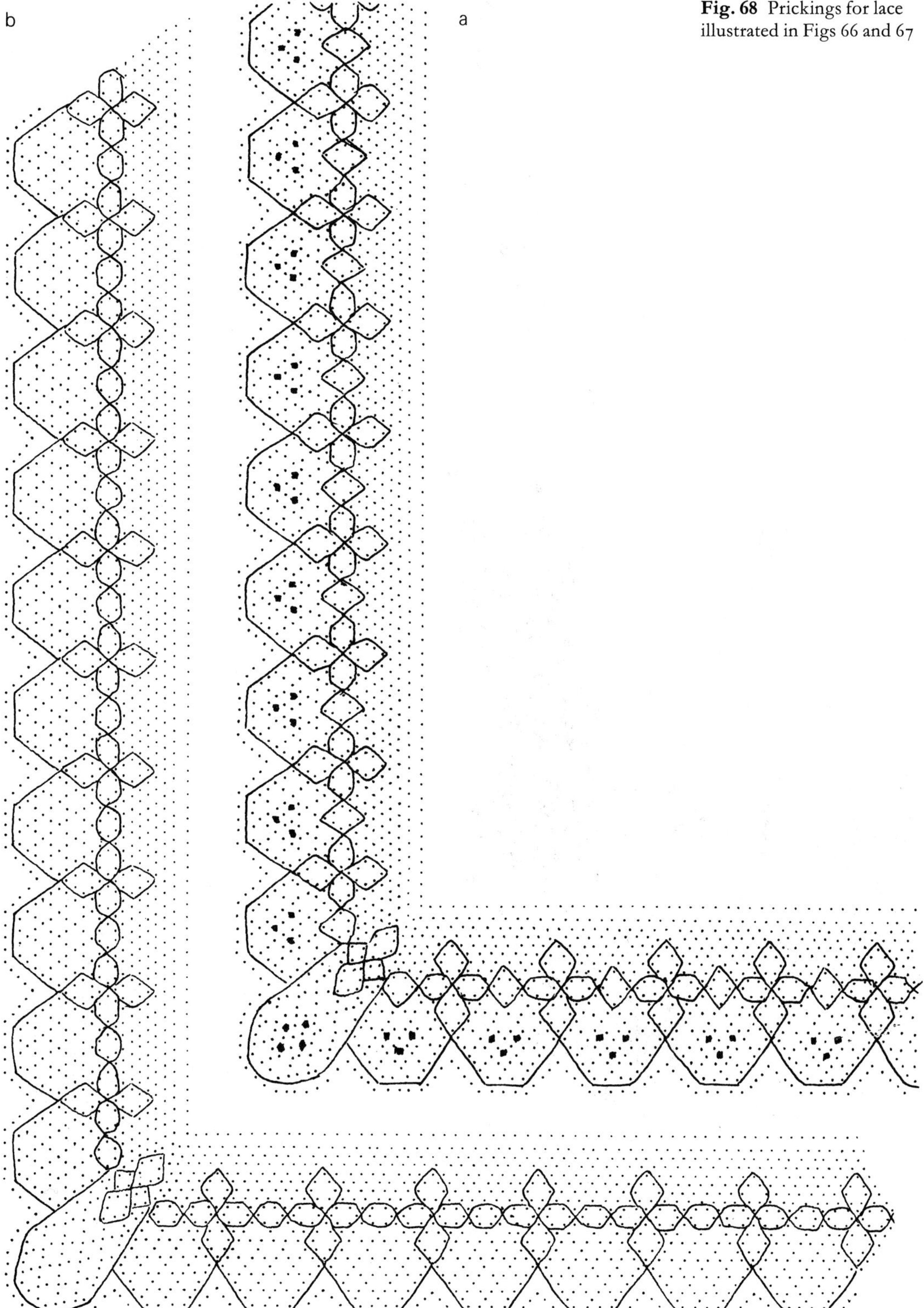

Fig. 68 Prickings for lace illustrated in Figs 66 and 67

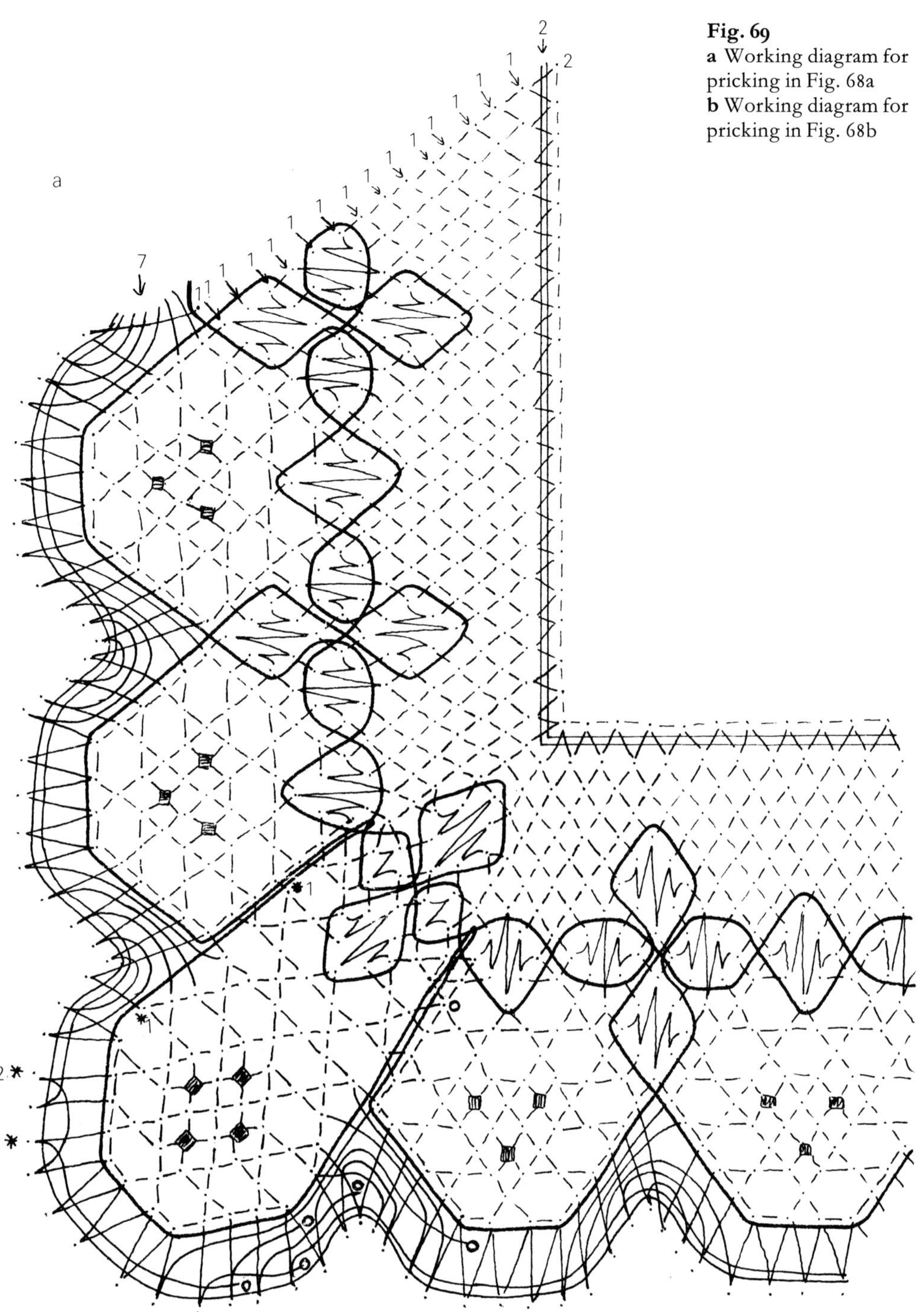

Fig. 69
a Working diagram for
pricking in Fig. 68a
b Working diagram for
pricking in Fig. 68b

the lace). Cut away the excess fabric from the hem at the back, close
to the stitching. This is less bulky than a double fold and allows for a
shaped hem.

Now attach the lace by flat overcasting. Seam the side edges

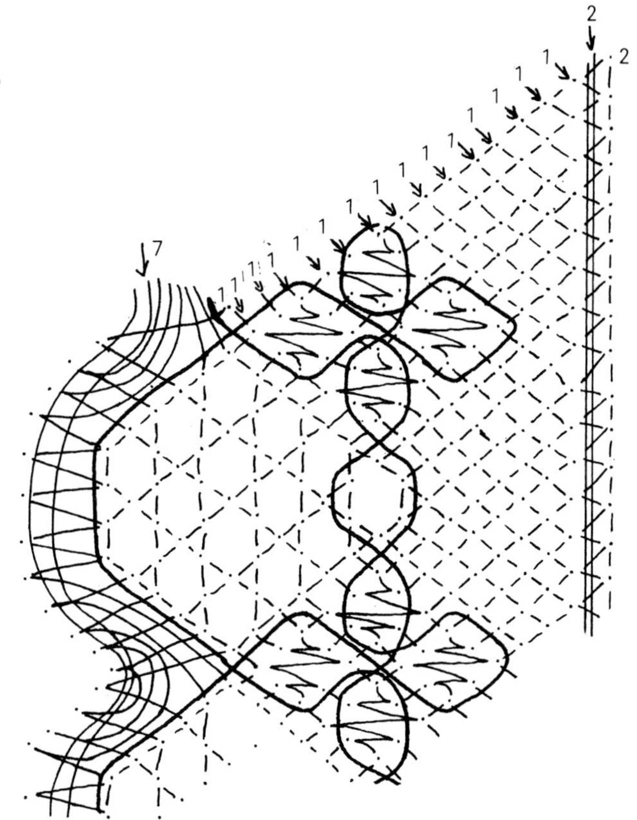

together – 1 cm (⅜ inch) seams are allowed – right sides facing, and press the seam open. Turn through to the right side and arrange the seam down the centre back. Press flat if a creased edge is required. Tack both layers together at the top and pleat them as indicated on the pattern, tacking the pleats into position. Prepare the second layer of the jabot in the same way. Place this on top of the first piece so that the hem will show, and cut off the top layer level at the top. Pleat the top in the same way, place both layers together and then bind the top with a straight strip of matching fabric as described on page 93.

The finished jabot can be pinned to a dress or blouse with a suitable brooch, or a pin may be stitched to the back and a small ribbon bow to the front.

Alternatives

1) The prickings and method of making the hem can also be used for a handkerchief. If a different pricking is used for the lace, the shape of the hem can be changed to echo either the edge of the lace or a feature of it.

2) These prickings could be used as an edging for a wedding veil and the prickings in Figs 47 or 49 could be used to make a head-dress (see page 65).

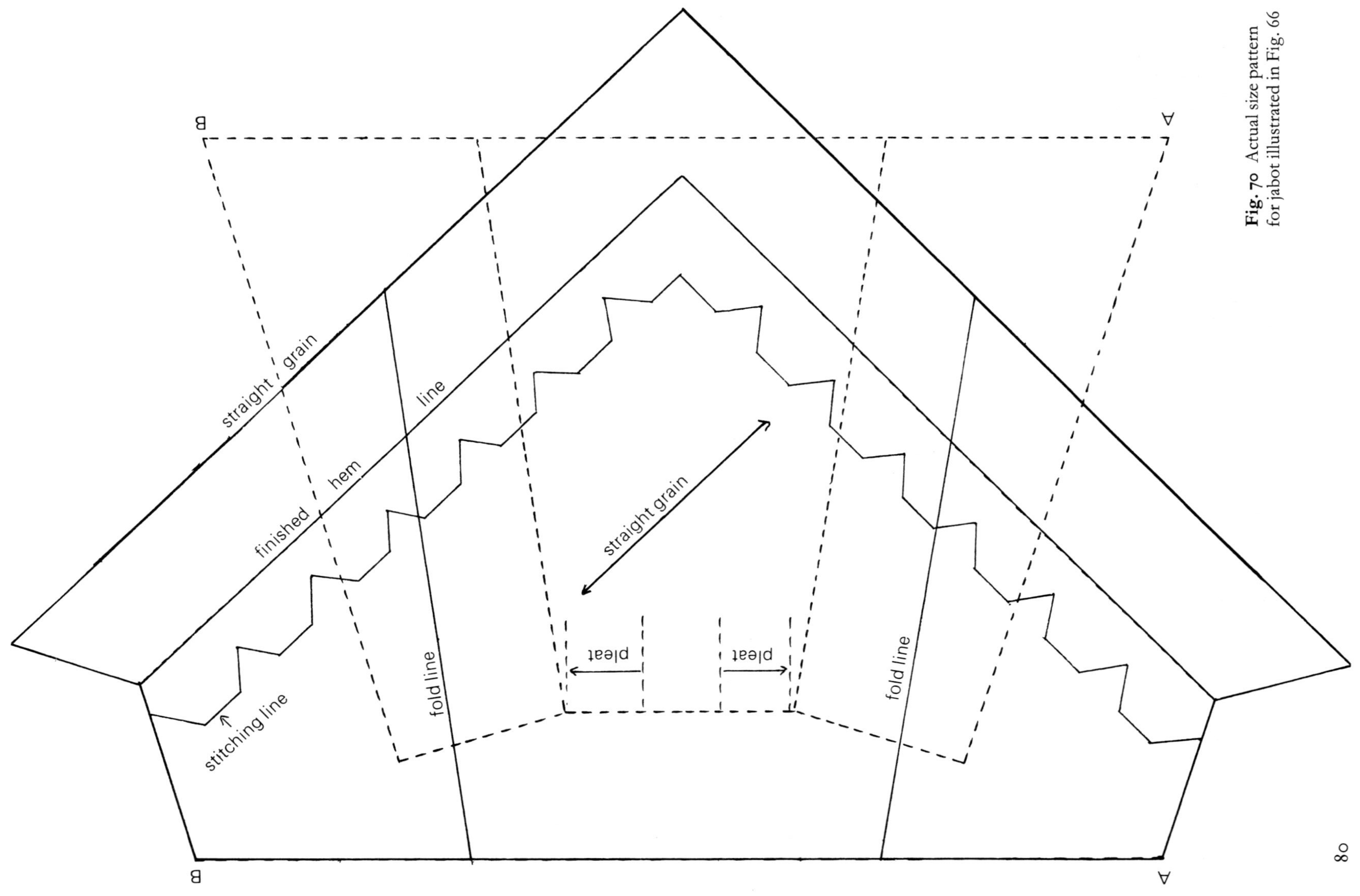

Fig. 70 Actual size pattern for jabot illustrated in Fig. 66

Clutch bag

This is a combination of lace and Trapunto and Italian quilting. The original was worked in a burnt-orange coloured thread and a synthetic thread with an opalescent effect in a slightly paler shade, mounted on a cream satin fabric.

This bag could be made in colours to match a bridesmaid's dress, and carried instead of a posy. It is illustrated in Fig. 71, and a detail of the lace and quilting shown in Fig. 72.

Fig. 71 Clutch bag

Fig. 72 Detail of lace and quilting on the clutch bag illustrated in Fig. 71

Materials	Tanne No. 50 – 26 pairs

Tanne No. 50 – 26 pairs
Supertwist No. 30 – 13 pairs
Piece of satin material, 75 cm (30 inches) by 46 cm (18 inches)
Piece of lining fabric, 75 cm (30 inches) by 46 cm (18 inches) – the original was slub rayon; choose a colour to match either the satin or the lace
Heavyweight interfacing 24.5 cm (9½ inches) by 48 cm (19 inches). The weight can be increased by ironing on a second or even a third layer of interfacing
Small amount of Dacron stuffing
Short length of quilting wool (or similar)
Small piece of muslin

The lace Referring to Figs 73 and 74, start a short way above the line **X–X**, which is the position of the seam line for the bag. The footside passives and the passives in both trails are Supertwist, and the scallop passives are Tanne No. 50. The edge pair, the footside weavers and the weavers for both trails are also Tanne No. 50, while the scallop weavers are Supertwist.

The working is straightforward, noting the connections of leaves to scallops and trails (see notes 3 and 4 on pages 11 and 12). Finish off by tying each pair in a reef knot.

The quilting All quilting techniques rely for their effect on the shadows cast, and therefore are best worked on a fairly soft fabric in a pale colour.

Place the satin on top of the muslin, making sure that the grain on each matches. Tack both layers together as shown in Fig. 38 and transfer the design on to the fabric, choosing a method which will not mark it permanently; I used tissue paper, which can be held in place with the same tacking. The design lines can then be marked by tacking stitches, or the quilting stitches can be worked directly; the tissue paper is then torn away. If running stitch is to be used for the quilting, the design can be drawn on to the backing fabric and the stitching worked from the wrong side.

Designs suitable for Italian quilting have a double outline which is worked in running stitch or back stitch. Complete the stitching, then, working from the back, thread the quilting wool into the channel formed by the stitching, leaving a small loop at any sharp turns in the design line to avoid pulling the wool too tight.

Designs for Trapunto quilting should enclose fairly small, shaped areas, which are outlined in back stitch or running stitch. When the stitching is completed, cut a small slit in the backing fabric (not the front) and push the stuffing in to pad out the shape. This slit is then closed by oversewing its edges together.

Making the bag The quilting should be worked before cutting out the fabric, as it tends to be 'shrunk' by quilting. The petal shapes are worked in Trapunto and the outline in Italian. A tiny matching bead was then sewn into the centre of the 'flower' shape.

Using the pattern given in Fig. 73, cut out as follows:
One piece lining
One piece interfacing (vilene plus iron-on vilene)
Three pieces top fabric (including the one on which the quilting
   has already been worked)

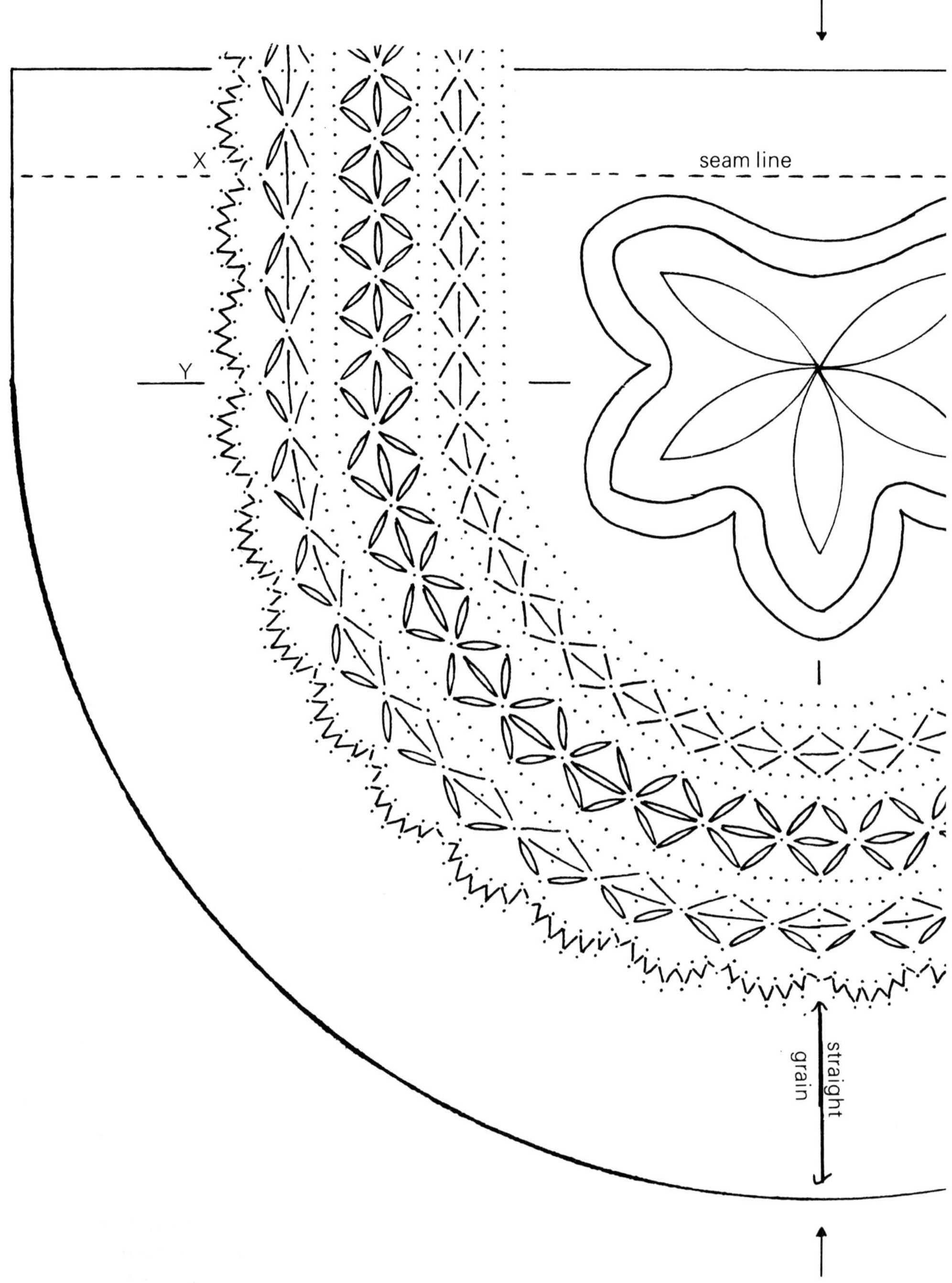

Fig. 73 Pricking and actual size pattern for lace and bag illustrated in Figs 71 and 72

Fold the pattern along the seam line. Place this fold to the fold of the
fabric and cut (from double fabric):
    One piece interfacing
    One piece lining
For the gusset, cut a bias strip 3.5 cm ($1\frac{3}{8}$ inches) wide and 40 cm

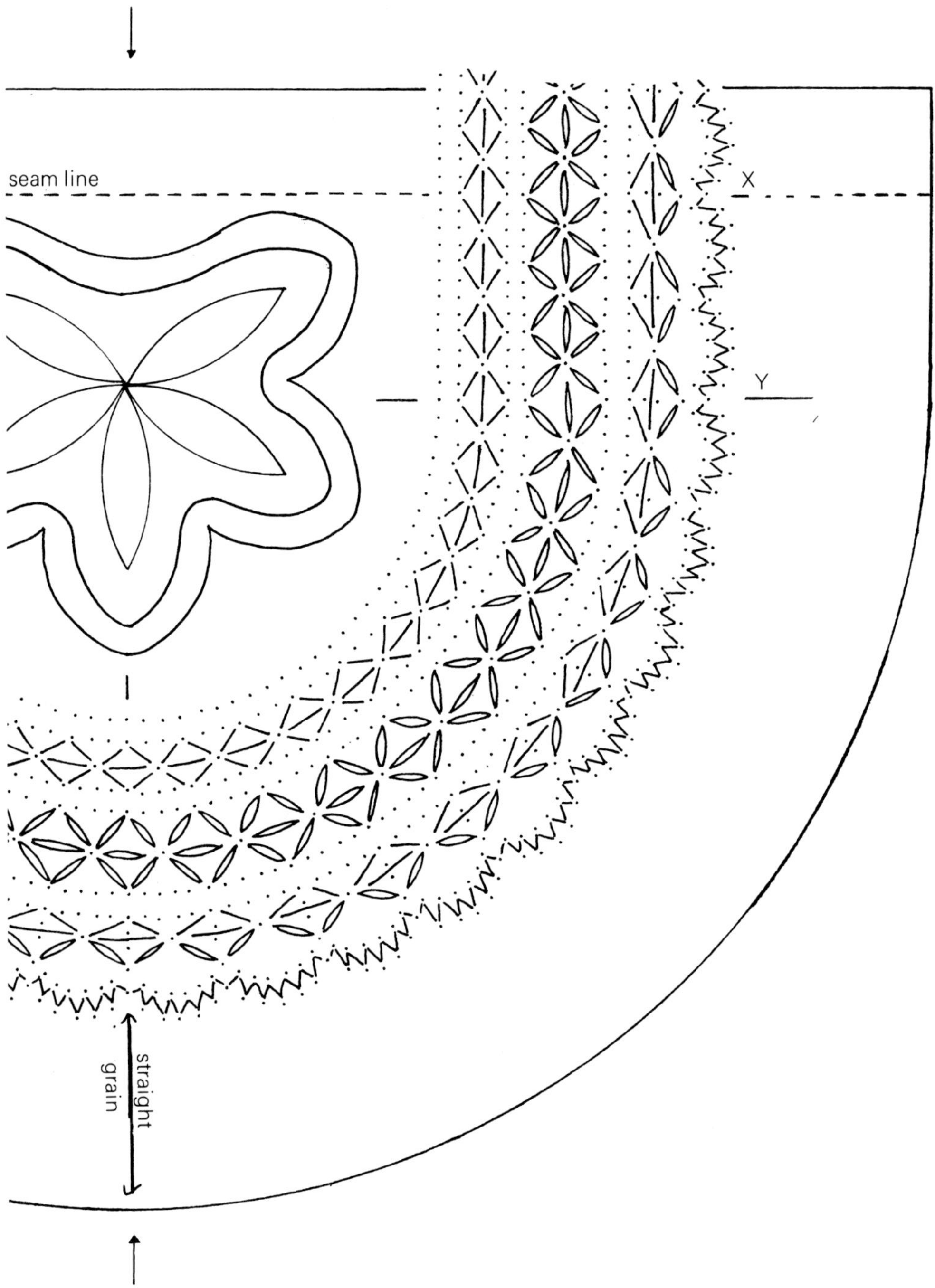

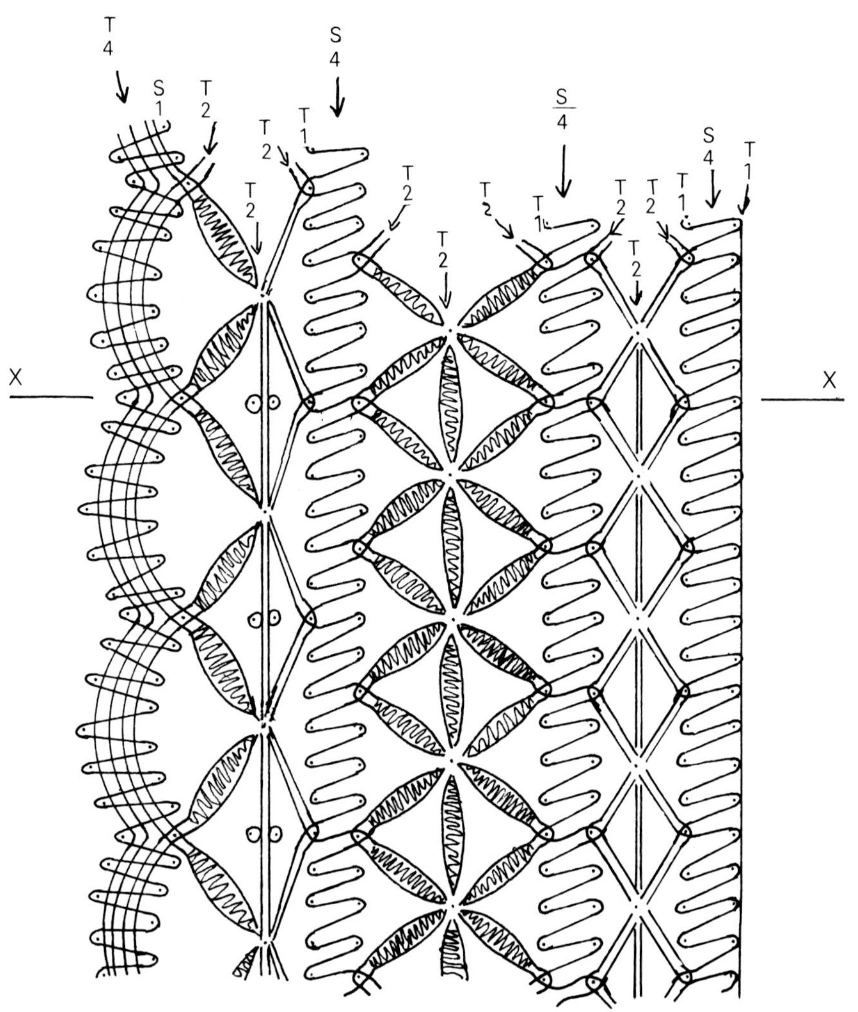

($15\frac{3}{4}$ inches) long from both lining and top fabric.

For the binding, cut bias strips 3 cm ($1\frac{3}{16}$ inch) wide and 40 cm ($15\frac{3}{4}$ inches) long, and 3 cm ($1\frac{3}{16}$ inches) wide and 80 cm ($31\frac{1}{2}$ inches) long from the top fabric.

For the front (i.e. pieces cut from the original pattern), tack the interfacing to the top fabric; then place the front and lining together, right sides facing, and seam along the straight edge. Trim off the excess interfacing, fold over and press so that the seam line lies along the top fold. Tack the curved edges together.

Place the two gusset pieces together, right sides facing, and seam both short ends. Turn through and press so that these seams lie at either end of the gusset. Now pin the gusset round the outer, curved edge of the front, with the seams in the front and the gusset level at the top and the linings facing each other. Fold the binding in half lengthwise (wrong sides facing) so that it is 15 mm ($\frac{5}{8}$ inch) wide and tuck in 1 cm ($\frac{3}{8}$ inch) at each end. Pin the binding to the front of the bag, right sides facing, then tack and machine it in place just 5 mm ($\frac{1}{5}$ inch) from the edge. Now fold the binding over towards the gusset to just cover the line of stitching and keep the bag front flat. Finally, stitch it neatly into place.

For the back and flap, first stitch the lace invisibly into place along both the foot and scalloped edges. Seam the two pieces cut from the top fabric along the straight edge and press the seam open, taking care not to flatten the quilting.

Place the lining, interfacing and top fabric together and tack all round. Pin the other edge of the gusset to the back of the bag, again lining up the seam lines and with the linings facing. Prepare the binding in the same way as before, joining on the straight grain to make the required length, and then pin the binding all round with the right sides of the top fabric and the binding facing each other. Open out the binding at the ends to seam them along the straight grain, choosing an inconspicuous place for the join – not on the front flap. Stitch the binding into place all round a bare 5 mm ($\frac{1}{5}$ inch) from the edge, then fold over to the inside/gusset and stitch in the same way as previously.

The bag is closed with either a press-stud or a velcro spot. A strap or cord could be added for use as a shoulder bag if desired.

Alternatives   This is a very adaptable pricking. If it is to be used as an edging or insertion, a heavier thread would be stronger – e.g. Brilliante d'Alsace No. 30 or Tanne No. 30. In this case use fewer pairs of passives in the foot, trails and scallops.

The following are a few suggestions:

1) Cutting the pricking along the line **Y–Y** gives a semicircle – use two for a circular mat.

2) Work a straight section between the two semicircular sections for either an oval mat (see Fig. 36) or a runner with rounded ends (*NB* **X–Y** is one complete pattern repeat, and Fig. 75 gives an additional length of the straight pricking).

3) Sections of the prickings in Figs 73 and 75 can be omitted, making an edge stitch on trails which will be attached to fabric. Consider some of the following ideas:

    a) Referring to Fig. 75, sections **A**, **B** and **C** can be used as insertions. Section **A** (three quarters of a circle) was worked in Brilliante d'Alsace No. 30 and inserted into the circular pocket illustrated on page 85 of *Mounting and Using Lace*.

    b) Sections **D** or **E** could be used as an edging.

Fig. 76 shows an idea for a hostess apron (or wedding apron). Make it from lawn and either finish the fabric edges by the double bias binding method or attach the lace directly with three-sided stitch. The ends of the lace will be concealed in the waistband. The same idea could also be adapted for a mat or tablecloth.

4) Other circular prickings of a suitable size could also be adapted to make the bag.

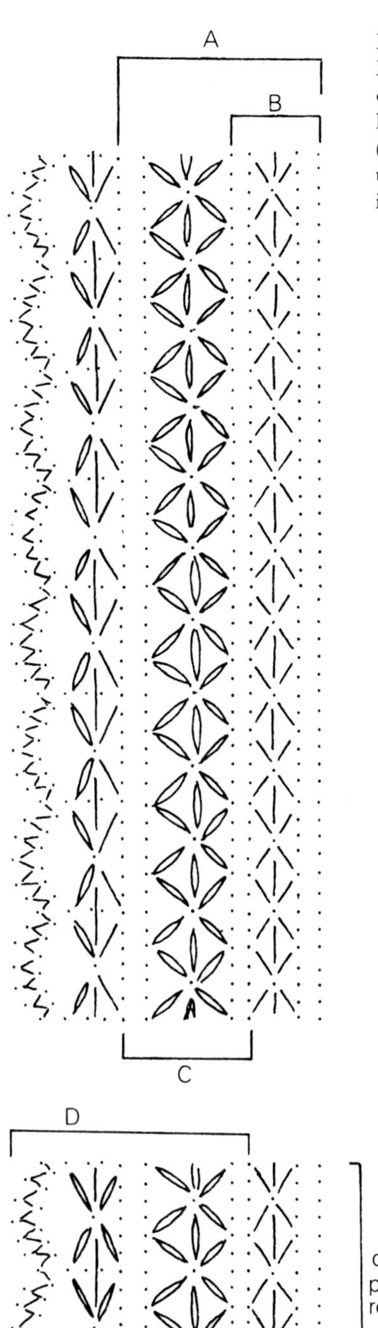

Fig. 75 Straight pricking for lace to match that illustrated on bag in Fig. 71. Also shows how sections of this pricking (or that in Fig. 73) can be used to make edgings and insertions of different widths

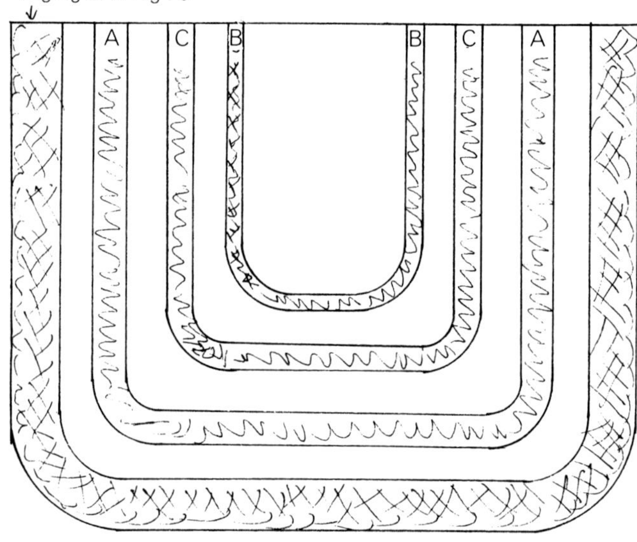

Fig. 76 Idea for a hostess apron using a variety of different sections of the prickings given in Figs 73 and 75

Collar with Torchon lace edging

Fig. 77 Collar with Torchon edging

This is a very adaptable pattern on which any suitable type of lace with a corner could be used. Choose a fabric of a weight suitable for the lace. All the straight edges are cut exactly on the straight grain of the fabric, and the collar hangs in a point at the back. The original was made in white, but the evenweave cotton used is available in other colours.

It is illustrated in Fig. 77, and a detail of the lace is shown in Fig. 78.

Fig. 80 Working diagram for pricking in Fig. 79

Fig. 79 Pricking for lace
illustrated in Figs 77 and 78

Materials	Tanne No. 30 – 15 pairs
	Perle No. 8 – 1 pair gimp
	Evenweave cotton (or other suitable fabric) with 27 threads to the inch, 40 cm (15¾ inches) square
	Tapestry needle No. 24

The lace The lace may be started along a straight edge and finished by tying each pair in a reef knot, because the ends will be covered by a binding. Fig. 80 illustrates the starting position if the lace is to be used for a continuous border where there must be a neat join.

To make the lace, refer to Figs 79 and 80; the working is straightforward. Fig. 81b shows the number of fans on each side of the finished collar. Remember to make an extra length at the beginning and end to enclose in the neck binding, and note that there are five corners.

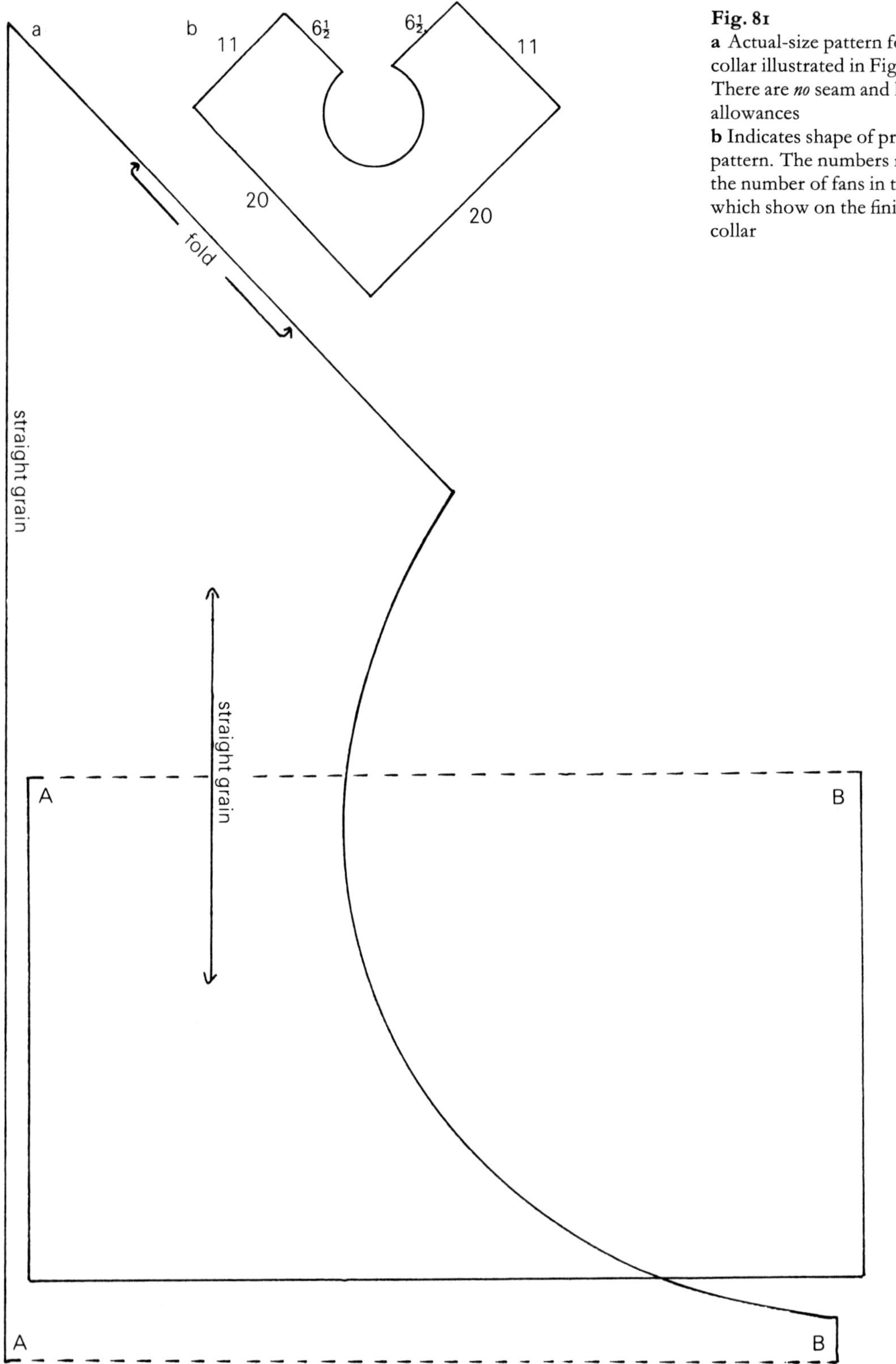

Fig. 81
a Actual-size pattern for collar illustrated in Fig. 77. There are *no* seam and hem allowances
b Indicates shape of prepared pattern. The numbers refer to the number of fans in the lace which show on the finished collar

Making up   Prepare the pattern given in Fig. 81a by tracing off both sections and joining them along the broken line **A–B**; no seams or hems are allowed, so these must be added. First, check the finished size against the lace and then add hem allowances on all the straight edges (except that marked *fold*), and a seam allowance on the curved edge. The finished hem on the collar illustrated is 1 cm ($\frac{3}{8}$ inch) deep, so add an extra 1.5 cm ($\frac{5}{8}$ inch) on the straight edges, and 1 cm ($\frac{3}{8}$ inch) seam allowance on the curved neck edge.

Cut this pattern from a folded piece of paper with the *fold* line against the fold in the paper, and then open it out flat. Fig. 81b shows the shape of this finished pattern; try it on to check that the neckline will fit correctly. Also check that the finished size will be correct for your lace; if it is not, adjust the position of the straight edges as necessary. When you are satisfied, cut the collar from a single layer of fabric, checking that each straight edge exactly follows the grain of the fabric.

Prepare a double-fold hem along all the straight edges, mitring all five corners and withdrawing a single thread all round for the hem stitch. Sew the hem in place with hem stitch and then flat overcast the lace to the collar.

Cut a bias strip of the evenweave fabric 3 cm ($1\frac{1}{4}$ inches) wide by 42 cm ($16\frac{1}{2}$ inches) long, joining it on the straight grain to obtain the required length. Pin the binding to the curved neck edge, right sides facing, with the binding extending 1 cm ($\frac{3}{8}$ inch) beyond the lace at each end. Stitch in place, clip the seam allowances and trim them to approximately 5 mm ($\frac{3}{16}$ inch). Turn under 1 cm ($\frac{3}{8}$ inch) at each end and 5 mm ($\frac{3}{16}$ inch) along the long edge. Fold the binding over to the wrong side to just cover the previous line of stitching, and stitch it neatly into place. The finished binding should be approximately 8 mm ($\frac{5}{16}$ inch) wide.

The collar may be fastened with a hook and bar on the ends of the binding. To disguise the binding at the front, pin or stitch a ribbon bow to the binding as illustrated in Fig. 77.

Alternatives   1) Make a more intricate drawn-thread work hem.
2) Add pulled work or counted-thread embroidery. If counted-thread embroidery is used, choose a coloured gimp for the lace to match the embroidery or make the lace in the same colour as the embroidery.
3) Use a finer fabric and stitch the hem into place with pin stitch, using a fine thread. The binding for the neckline could be extended to make ties, but this requires extra fabric.
4) Attach a fine lace directly to a fine fabric with three-sided stitch. A wider lace could be used, adjusting the size of the fabric so that the completed collar remains about the same size.
5) Make the collar from double fabric.

Blouse with motifs on sleeves

Fig. 82 Blouse with motifs on sleeves

This idea is equally suitable for either a home-made or ready-made garment, although it would be easier to apply the motifs and work the embroidery before the sleeves are made up. The original blouse was made in a chestnut-brown polyester cotton fabric and the lace was worked in a lemon-coloured thread. Make sure that your chosen thread and fabric will wash together satisfactorily.

The blouse is illustrated in Fig. 82, and a detail of the lace is shown in Fig. 83.

Fig. 84 Pricking for large motif illustrated in Figs 82 and 83

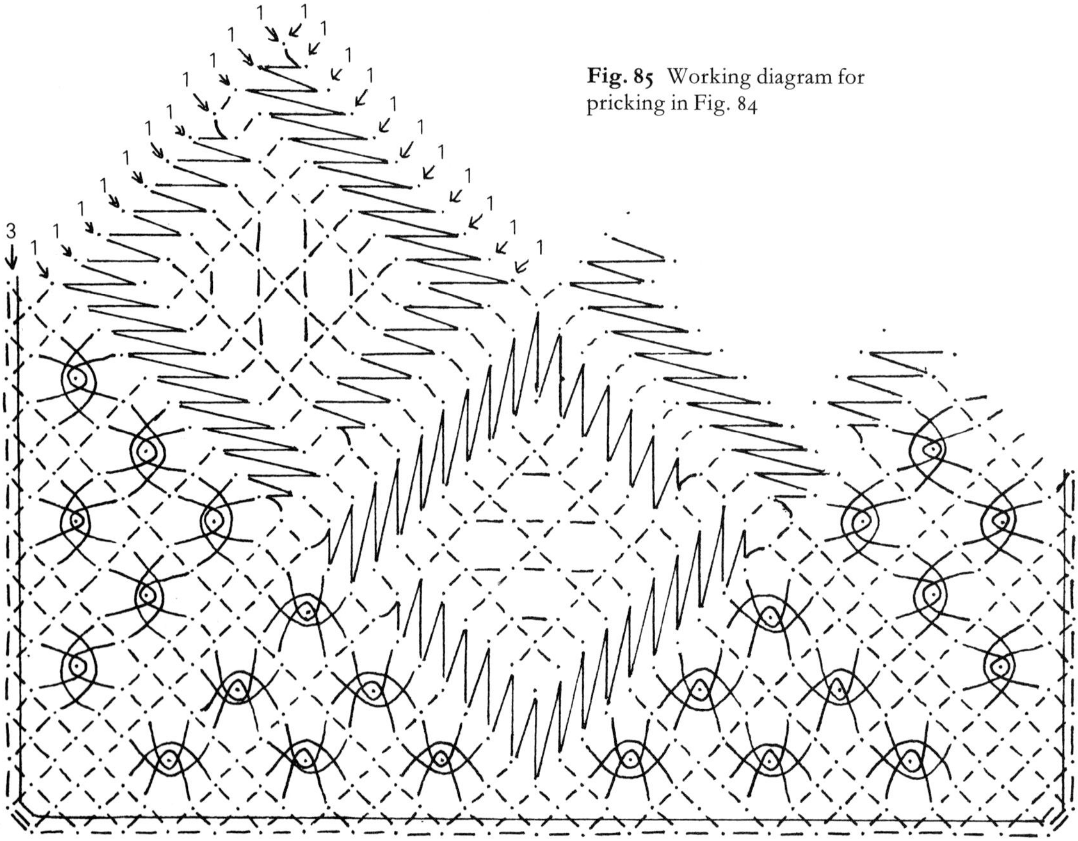

Fig. 85 Working diagram for pricking in Fig. 84

96

Blouse with motifs on sleeves

Two lampshades and place
setting

Fig. 86 Pricking for small
motif illustrated in Figs 82
and 83

Fig. 87 Working diagram for
pricking in Fig. 86. The lines
A–A cut the corners

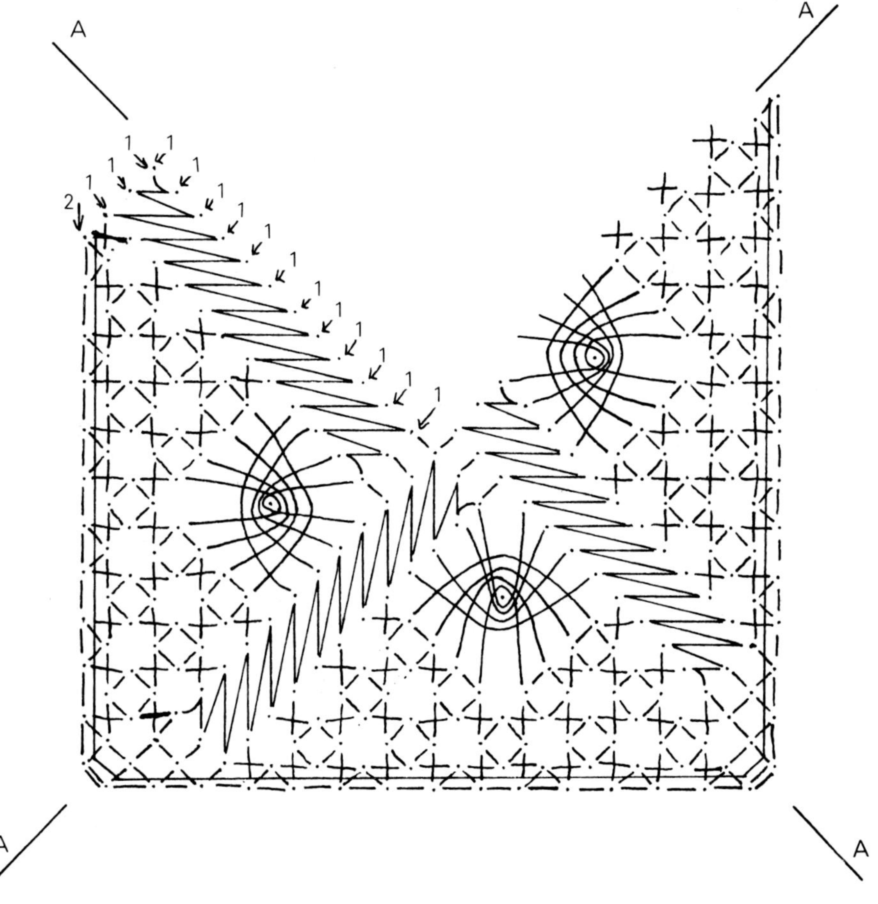

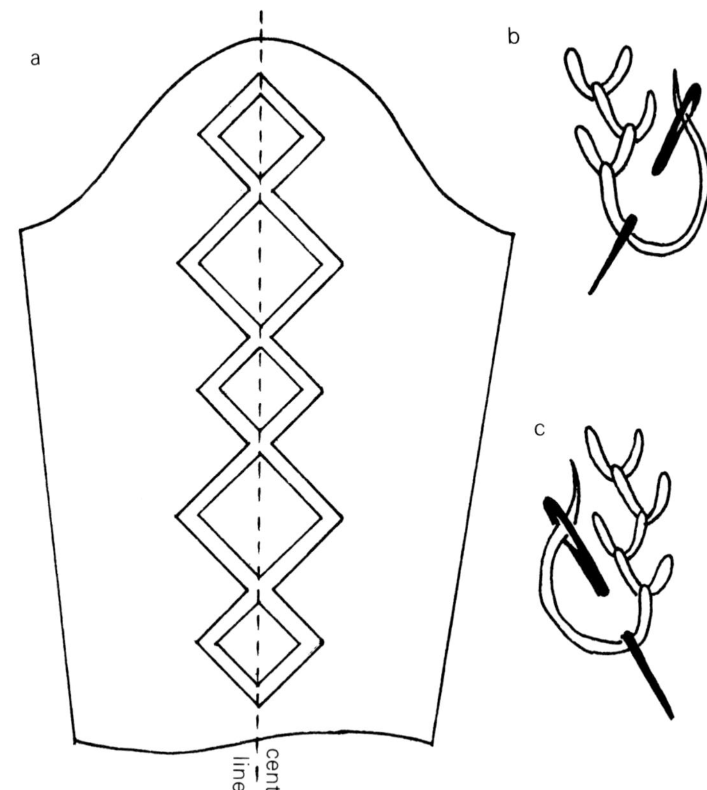

Fig. 88
a Placing motifs on sleeve
b and **c** Feather stitch

Materials Tanne No. 50 – 25 pairs for the pricking in Fig. 84 and 17 pairs for the pricking in Fig. 86
Appropriate fabric (or blouse)
Stranded embroidery cotton

The lace These motifs are worked in triangular sections, not from top to bottom – notice where they are started for a neat join. Referring to Figs 84 and 85 for the larger motif, and 86 and 87 for the smaller one, work the lace, starting where indicated. When completed, darn in all the ends before applying the lace to the blouse. Most pairs may be darned into the cloth stitch, leaving only the edge pairs (two pairs on the small motif and three pairs on the large motif) which may be formed into a roll and stitched carefully behind the edge passive pair.

   N.B.   On the *small* motif, when working the rose ground notice that the intervening stitches are omitted when going into and coming out of the spider.

The blouse

Make as usual except for the sleeves, which should not be cut out at this stage. I replaced the top-stitching on the yoke with feather stitch worked in two strands of the stranded cotton in order to echo the sleeve and give a link between it and the rest of the blouse (see Fig. 88b and c).

Mounting the lace

Check that the length of the sleeve pattern is correct and adjust at this stage if necessary. Tack the outline of the sleeve on to the fabric but do not cut out yet. Mark the centre line (see page 109) down the sleeve with tacking stitches.

Place the lace motifs as shown in Fig. 88a, adjusting their exact spacing to suit the length of the sleeve – on the original the points of the motifs were 1.5 cm ($\frac{5}{8}$ inch) apart – and pin them into place. If the embroidery is to be worked in a frame, tack round each motif to mark its position and then remove; if it is to be worked in the hand, the motifs may be invisibly stitched all round into place at this stage.

Using small tacking stitches, mark the line for the embroidery (which 'ties' the motifs together and prevents a 'stuck-on' appearance). I marked the line 1 cm ($\frac{3}{8}$ inch) out from the motifs and then worked feather stitch (see Fig. 88b and c) using two strands of the stranded cotton, just *inside* this line. Start at the top point and work one side, then start the other side in the same place; this ensures that the stitches travel in the same direction on both sides. I used a thread in a colour to match the fabric, but one to match the lace could be used instead.

Other suitable line stitches could be used for this outline and on the yoke. If the fabric is suitable, the outline could be worked in a pulled stitch such as pin stitch or four-sided stitch.

Now stitch the motifs in place invisibly (if this has not already been done) and then cut out and make up the sleeve.

Alternatives

1) Different shapes and types of motifs could be used in the same way.

2) The motifs could be made to match the fabric and inserted – they will still benefit from an outline of stitching. Pin stitch or four-sided stitch may be best in this case.

3) Insert motifs (of a matching colour) and then back them with a contrasting coloured fabric which could be held in place with the decorative stitching that is needed for completeness.

4) For a more formal occasion, make a jabot as described on page 74 using a suitable Torchon pricking with thread and fabric to match the lace on the sleeve.

5) The motifs may be used in other ways, for example:

   a) The small motif could be applied or inserted into a handkerchief corner

   b) The small motif could be used in a paperweight

   c) The large motif could be applied to or inserted in a cushion.

Fig. 89a illustrates five motifs applied or inserted, and surrounded by a line of embroidery, Italian quilting or drawn-thread work. Fig. 89b uses only one motif, with bands of drawn-thread work, into which 1.5 mm ($\frac{1}{16}$ inch) embroidery ribbon could also be threaded. It could be enlarged and worked in a coarser thread for this purpose. Similar ideas could be used to make a pram or cot cover.

Fig. 89 Two ideas for using lace motifs on a cushion cover

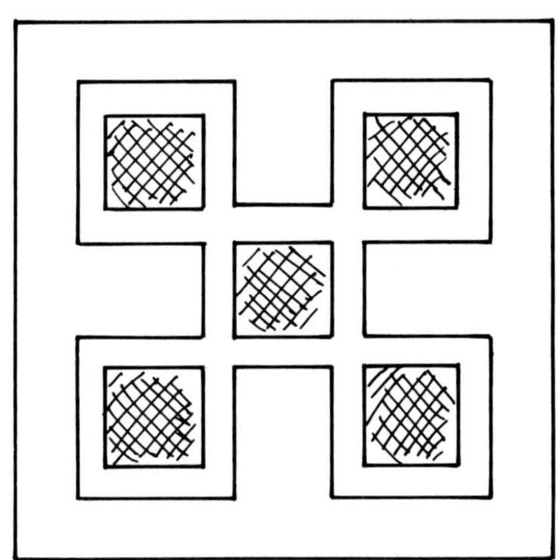

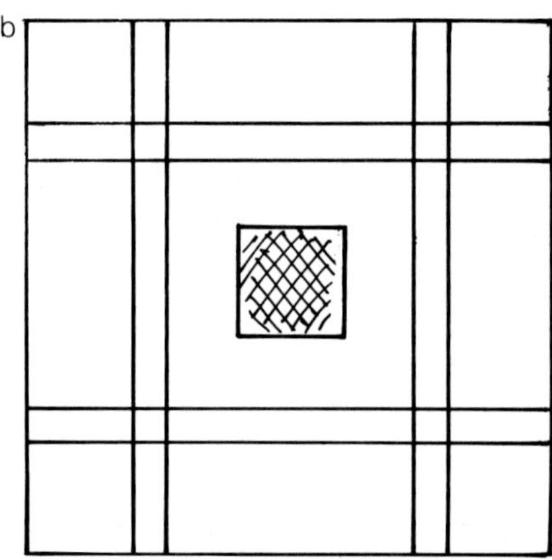

Bookmark in Beds/Maltese-type lace

Fig. 90 Bookmark and lace
for button

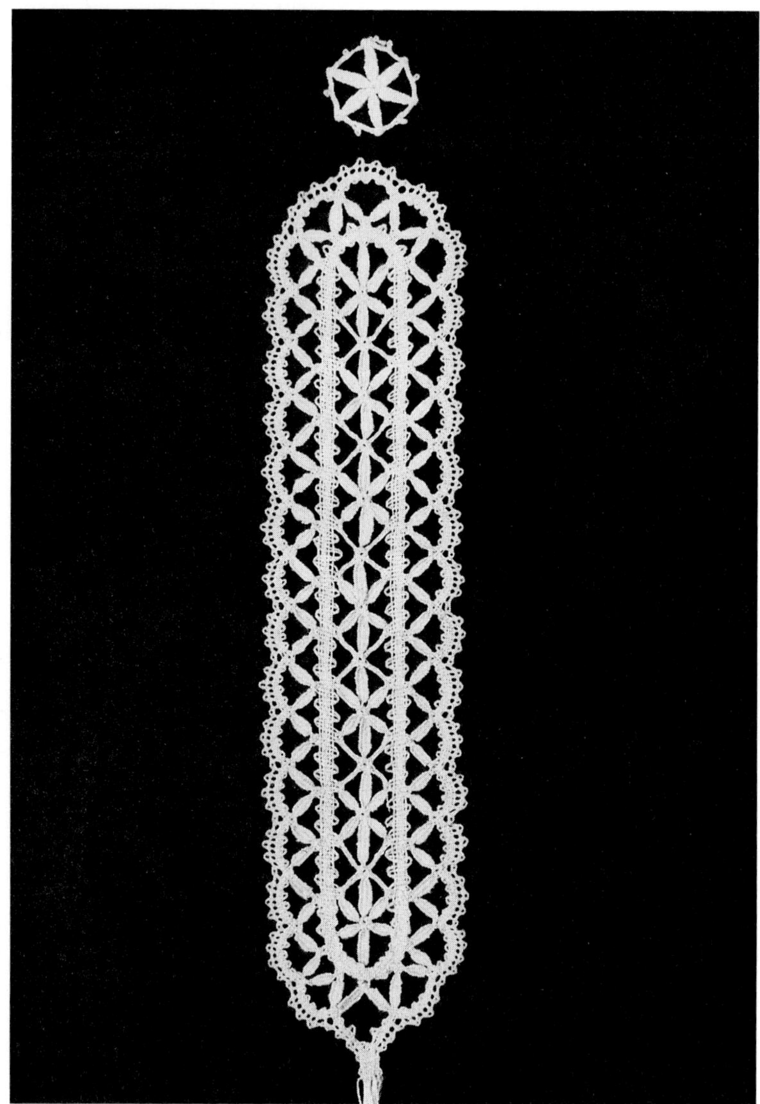

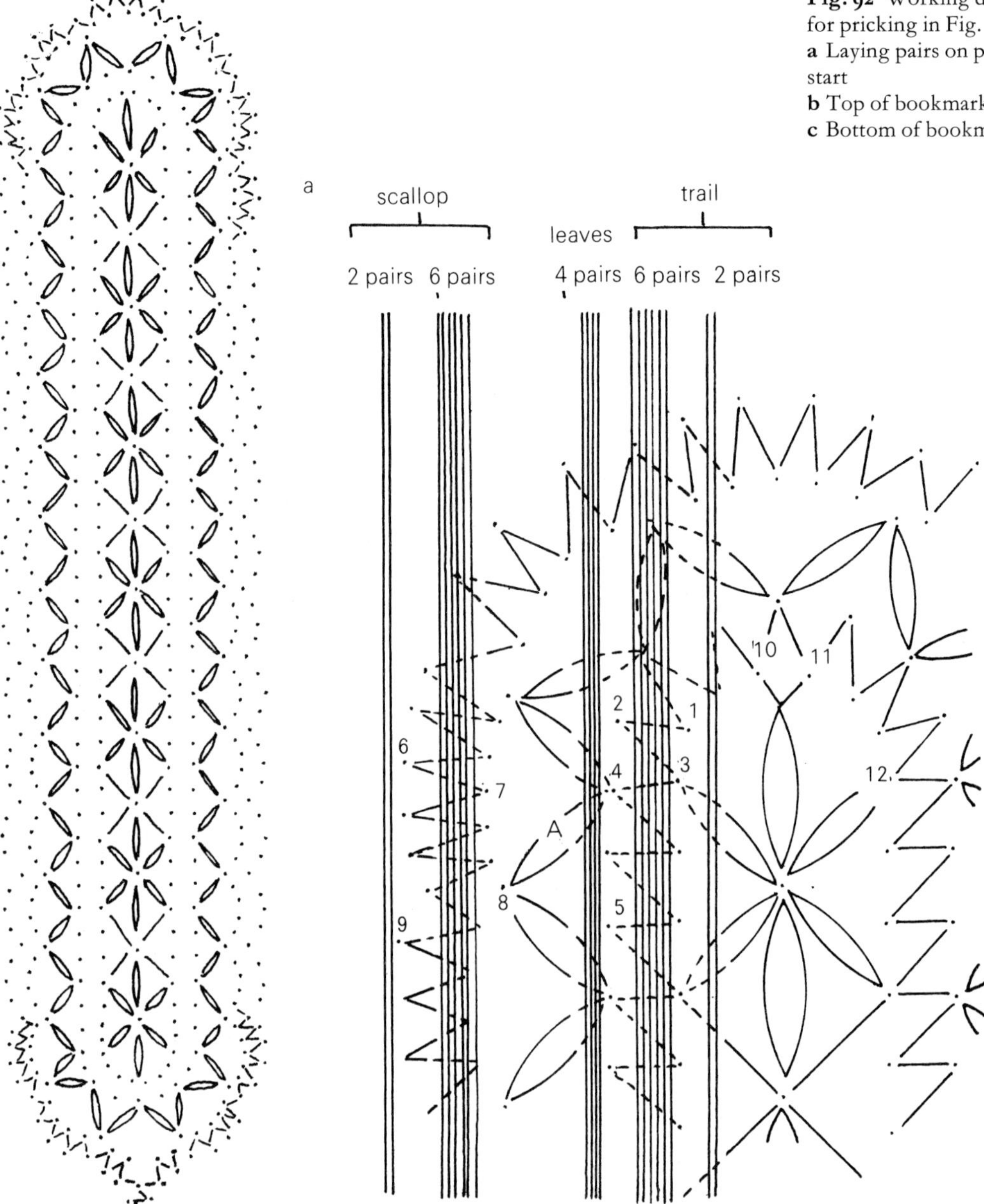

Fig. 91 Pricking for bookmark illustrated in Fig. 90

Fig. 92 Working diagrams for pricking in Fig. 91:
a Laying pairs on pillow to start
b Top of bookmark
c Bottom of bookmark

The bookmark is shown in Fig. 90.

Materials   Tanne No. 30 – 26 pairs

The lace   Referring to Figs 91 and 92a, start on the left-hand side of the bookmark with the cloth stitch trail. Set pin 1 and then lay eight pairs of bobbins across the pillow from front to back as indicated in

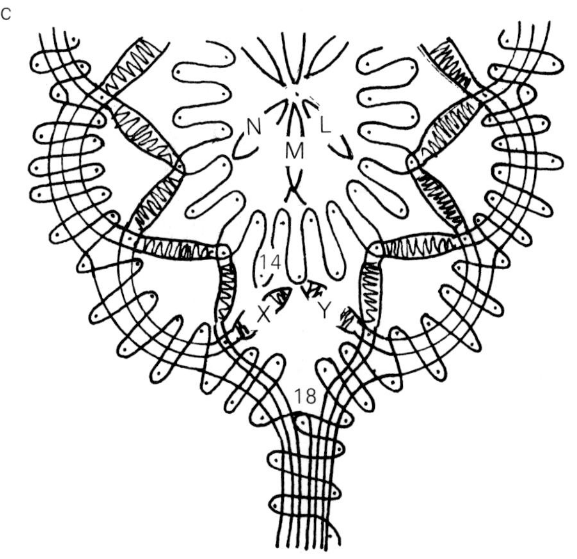

Fig. 92a where each line represents *one thread*. Pin the bobbins at the back of the pillow down firmly with a piece of elastic and use only the bobbins at the front. Use the two bobbins to the right of pin 1 as weavers, and work them in cloth stitch through three pairs to pin 2, then back to pin 3 where two pairs are introduced for a leaf (see note 5 on page 12).

Now lay four pairs from front to back of the pillow to the left of the trail (see Fig. 92a – leaf pairs) and connect the two pairs at the front to the trail at pin 4 (see note 3 on page 11). Continue the trail as far as pin 5, then make leaf **A**.

The scalloped edge is started by setting pin 6 and laying eight pairs across the pillow from front to back as shown in Fig. 92a. Use the two bobbins to the left of pin 6 as weavers, and work the scallop connecting leaf **A** at pin 8 (see note 4 on page 12). Then work as far as pin 9 – note that the edge passives of the scallop are worked in whole stitch and twist (double half stitch).

Now turn the pillow through 180 degrees and use the bobbins which were left at the back to work round the top of the bookmark, gradually turning the pillow as you work and referring to Fig. 92b. Add one pair at each of pins 10 and 11 and two pairs at pin 12. When the right-hand side of the bookmark has been reached, continue working straight down the pattern.

Referring to Fig. 92c, continue the left-hand trail as far as pin 14, having taken out the pairs from leaf **N** (see note 6 on page 13), but do *not* set pin 14 yet. On the right-hand side take out the pairs from leaves **L** and **M** in the same way and continue round to pin 14 but still do not set pin 14. Do not make leaves **X** and **Y** yet.

Taking one bobbin from each side of the trail, in order, tie them together in a reef knot and lay to the back. Tie all the trail passives in this way, then set pin 14. Now tie the trail weavers in front of pin 14 in the same way and lay back.

The leaves **X** and **Y** can now be made and the pairs sewn in and tied. Continue with the scallops on both sides until they meet at pin 18 and then work three or four rows in cloth stitch. Tie each pair from the scallops in a reef knot and cut off to form a fringe. All other ends of thread can either be cut off close to the lace, or, for extra strength, be darned in.

Blouse with epaulettes

Fig. 93 Blouse with epaulettes

The blouse pattern used was a simple shirt style with a shoulder seam and without a yoke; the adaptation necessary to include a yoke is given below. If you wish to add the decorative flaps, do not use a pattern where the front is gathered or pleated into the yoke, as the flaps would not lie flat.

The instructions for the added epaulettes are given below; they are trimmed with lace worked on the same pricking as the bookmark (Fig. 91). The blouse is finished with a concealed button band in order not to detract from the epaulettes and flaps, and is illustrated in Fig. 93. Details of the lace are illustrated in Fig. 90.

The original blouse was made in apricot-coloured polyester cotton with pale green lace and was designed to be worn with the skirt illustrated on page 85 of *Mounting and Using Lace*, which was made in pale green with apricot-coloured fabric behind the inserted lace.

Materials   Tanne No. 30 – 26 pairs (for the epaulettes)
Tanne No. 30 – 8 pairs (for the buttons)
Two 19 mm-diameter button moulds
Suitable material, interfacing and pattern for the blouse

The lace   The working method is given for the bookmark (see page 102). For the epaulette, work as for the bookmark, making the length required and finally tying each pair of threads together in a reef knot and cut off; all these ends will be concealed in the collar seam, making it unnecessary to shape this end.

Making the blouse   The blouse is made up in the usual way except for the following adaptations.

To prepare the front yoke pattern, cut the pattern for the front at right angles to the centre front line in the required position – on the blouse illustrated this was 3.5 cm ($1\frac{3}{8}$ inches) below the front neck edge. Add seam allowances to both pieces – if these are very generous the position of the seam can be adjusted to suit when trying on. The flaps are semicircles 9 cm ($3\frac{1}{2}$ inches) in diameter, with seam allowances added all round. Cut two pieces of fabric and one piece of interfacing for each flap and seam the circular edges; clip, turn, and press them. Top stitch round the curved edge, 6 mm ($\frac{1}{4}$ inch) from the edge, before tacking into place in the yoke seam – on the original these were 8 cm ($3\frac{1}{4}$ inches) in from the front edge, but try your blouse on to decide the exact position. They are decorated with a lace-trimmed button (described below).

The epaulettes are 4.5 cm ($1\frac{3}{4}$ inches) wide with one end semicircular. When making the pattern, adjust its length to fit the shoulder seam of the blouse and add turnings all round. Using this pattern, for each epaulette cut two pieces from the fabric and one from the interfacing; invisibly stitch the lace into place, taking care that it is placed centrally on the fabric. Interface the epaulette and sew the two pieces together, right sides facing, leaving the straight end open. Clip the seams, turn and press. Pin the epaulettes to the shoulder seam and attach the collar, thus fixing the epaulettes in place; then make one or two invisible stitches through its rounded end and the shoulder seam to hold it in place. The collar points were also rounded off to 'match' the flaps and epaulettes.

The buttons Referring to Figs 94 and 95, make the lace; the pairs for the three leaves are introduced at 'windmill' crossings. To take out the pairs from each leaf, make a 'windmill' crossing and then tie the leaf pairs. There are now two possible methods of working, each of which has its own advantages and disadvantages.

For the first method, make a roll of threads behind the appropriate leaves; this is most easily achieved by using a fine bent needle whilst the lace is still pinned down on the pillow. Now cover the button mould with the blouse fabric and stitch the lace invisibly into place. Working in this way enables the lace to be easily positioned accurately but does require all the ends of thread to be finished first.

The alternative is to attach the lace to the fabric, taking all the ends of thread through to the wrong side and then covering the button mould. The ends of thread are more easily dealt with using this method, but it is difficult to position the lace in the correct place on the finished button; I used the first method when making the original.

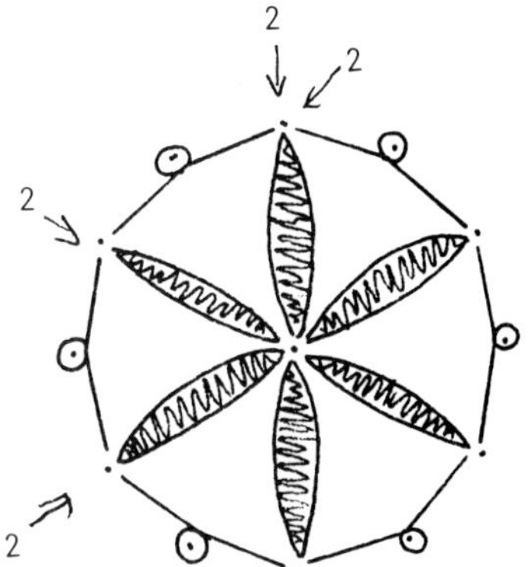

Fig. 94 Pricking for lace on button illustrated in Figs 90 and 93

Fig. 95 Working diagram for pricking in Fig. 94

Alternatives 1) Other bookmark patterns could be used in this way. If the end of the lace is pointed, make the epaulette pointed; if the lace has a square end, then so should the epaulette. Cut the decorative flaps pointed or square, to match the epaulette. If your figure permits, the decorative flaps could be replaced with patch pockets and flaps.

2) A strip of the same lace could be applied to the centre front of a blouse where a concealed button band has been used.

Blouse with pleated sleeves

Fig. 96 Blouse with pleated sleeves worn with jabot (see page 70)

Whilst a narrow Bucks Point-type edging was used for the blouse illustrated (see Figs 96 and 97), any narrow pricking could be used. A fine Torchon lace, possibly including a gimp thread, would look equally attractive. Simple laces are often far more effective in this type of situation than more complicated ones.

Check that your chosen thread and fabric will wash together; the original was made in a cream synthetic satin and the lace in a pale peach-coloured cotton. The original pattern used for the blouse did not have a pleat in the sleeve; the adaptation for this is given below. Make the lace before adapting the sleeve pattern but after checking the required length of the sleeve.

Materials

Tanne No. 50 – 20 pairs
Coton à Broder No. 25 – 1 pair (gimp)
Suitable fabric and pattern for the blouse
Stranded embroidery cotton to match the lace

The lace

The ends will not show, therefore the starting position is unimportant; to finish, each pair may be tied in a reef knot and cut off. The pricking is given in Fig. 98 and the working method shown in Fig. 99; if the lace is started as in the drawing, then a neat join can be achieved if it is required. Four pieces of lace, each the length of the sleeve from shoulder to cuff, will be needed.

Making the sleeves

First, make a copy of your sleeve pattern, transferring all the information (i.e. balance marks, grain, slit etc.); this copy will be used to make the necessary adaptations.

Draw in the centre line, which is found by folding the pattern in half. This fold should be parallel to the grain line, and the pattern is then cut along this line (see Fig. 100a).

Measure the width of the lace – 2.2 cm ($\frac{7}{8}$ inch) on the original; do *not* measure the pricking as this can be slightly different. Draw a line this distance from the cut edge on both pattern pieces (see Fig. 100b); this will be the *fold* line and should be labelled clearly on your pattern pieces. Now decide on the depth of the finished pleat – also 2.2 cm ($\frac{7}{8}$ inch) on the original, but it need not necessarily be the same – and draw a line this distance out from the fold line to establish the seam line (see Fig. 100c). On the original, this line was the same as the original centre line.

Now add a seam allowance, 1.5 cm ($\frac{5}{8}$ inch), to the pleat edge of both pattern pieces. Fold the patterns along the fold line and cut the top edge of the pleat portion to follow the original sleeve head line and the lower edge to follow the original curve. Next prepare the pattern for the pleat underlay; calculate the width of the underlay, which is:

Twice the width of the lace (i.e. 2 × 2.2 cm = 4.4 cm)
Plus twice the depth of the pleat (2 × 2.2 cm = 4.4 cm)
Plus twice the seam allowance (2 × 1.5 cm = 3 cm)
So the total width is 4.4 cm + 4.4 cm + 3 cm = 11.8 cm

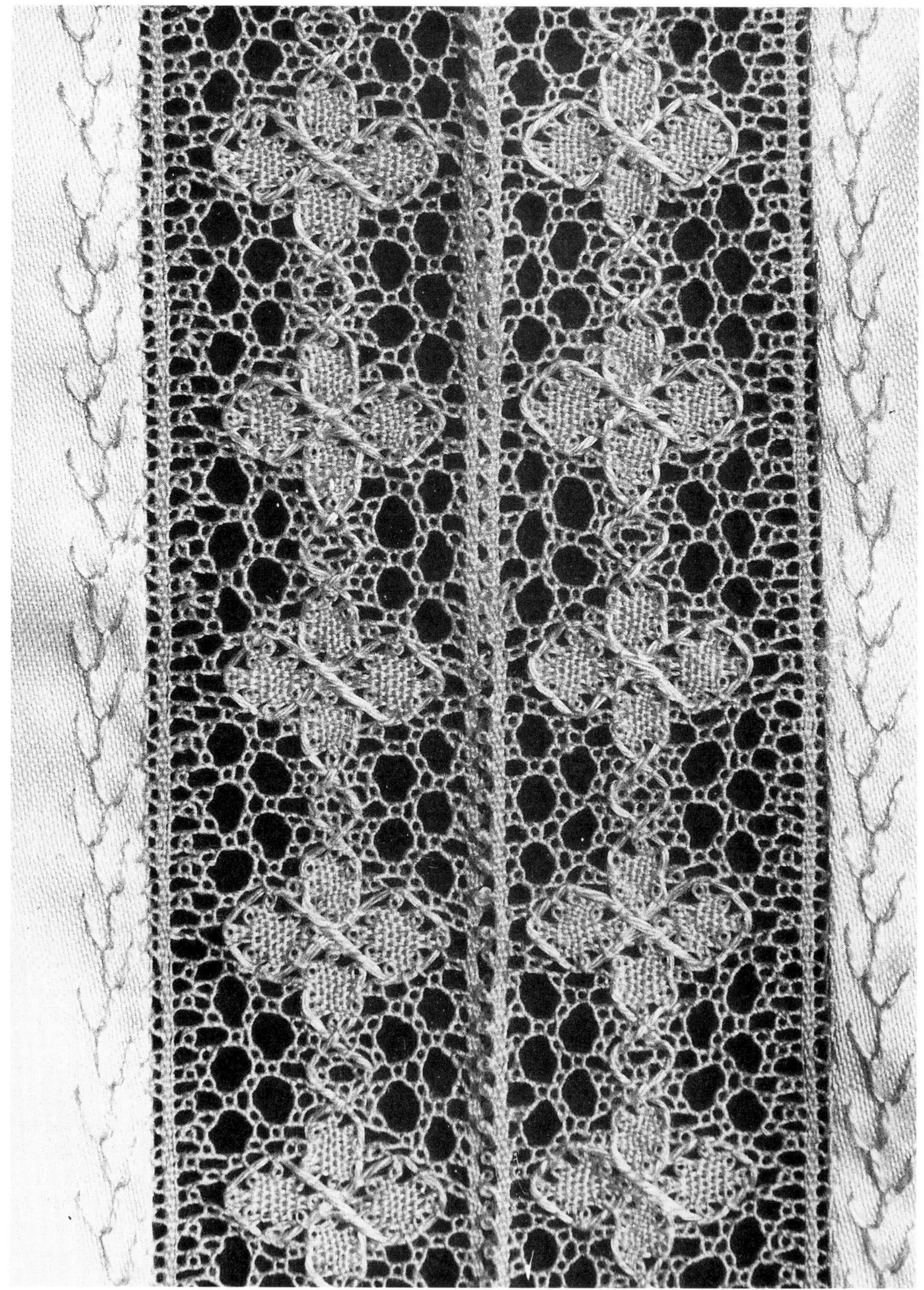

Fig. 97 Detail of lace on blouse illustrated in Fig. 96. The picot edges just touch but are *not* joined to each other

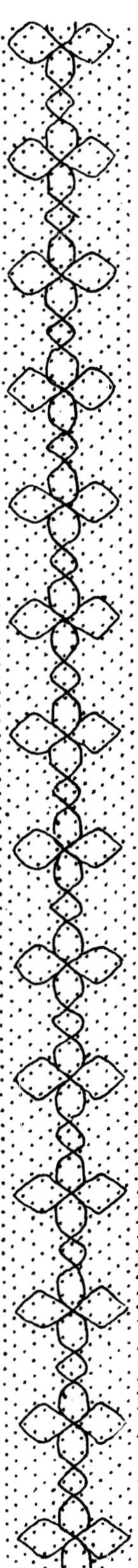

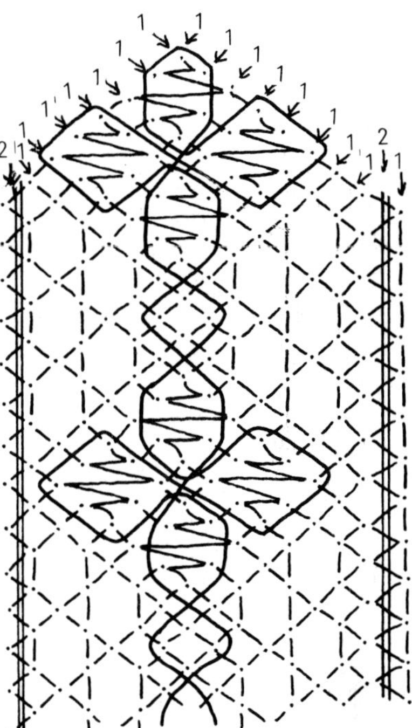

Fig. 98 Pricking for lace
illustrated in Figs 96 and 97

Fig. 99 Working diagram for
pricking in Fig. 98

Cut a strip of paper this width and slightly longer than your
original sleeve pattern. Draw a line down the centre of this strip and
then place it under your original pattern with this line matching the
centre line. Draw in the curves for the top and bottom edges and cut
the shape out (see Fig. 100d).

Your pattern is now ready; cut out following the diagram in Fig.
100e.

To make up the sleeve, press the pleat and its seam allowance
under along the fold line. In order to give a firm edge to which to
attach the lace, a line of stitching must be worked along the edge
through both layers of fabric to hold the fold in place. If the fabric is
suitable, pin stitch would be a good choice; however, on the satin I
used feather stitch (see Figs 88b and c) which was worked in a single
strand of stranded embroidery cotton to match the lace. The lace
may then be flat overcast into place on the folded edge from the
wrong side. Now join the pleat underlay to each side of the sleeve;
tack through the pleats at top and bottom along the seam lines to
hold them in place while the sleeve is completed and inserted in the
usual way (see Fig. 100f).

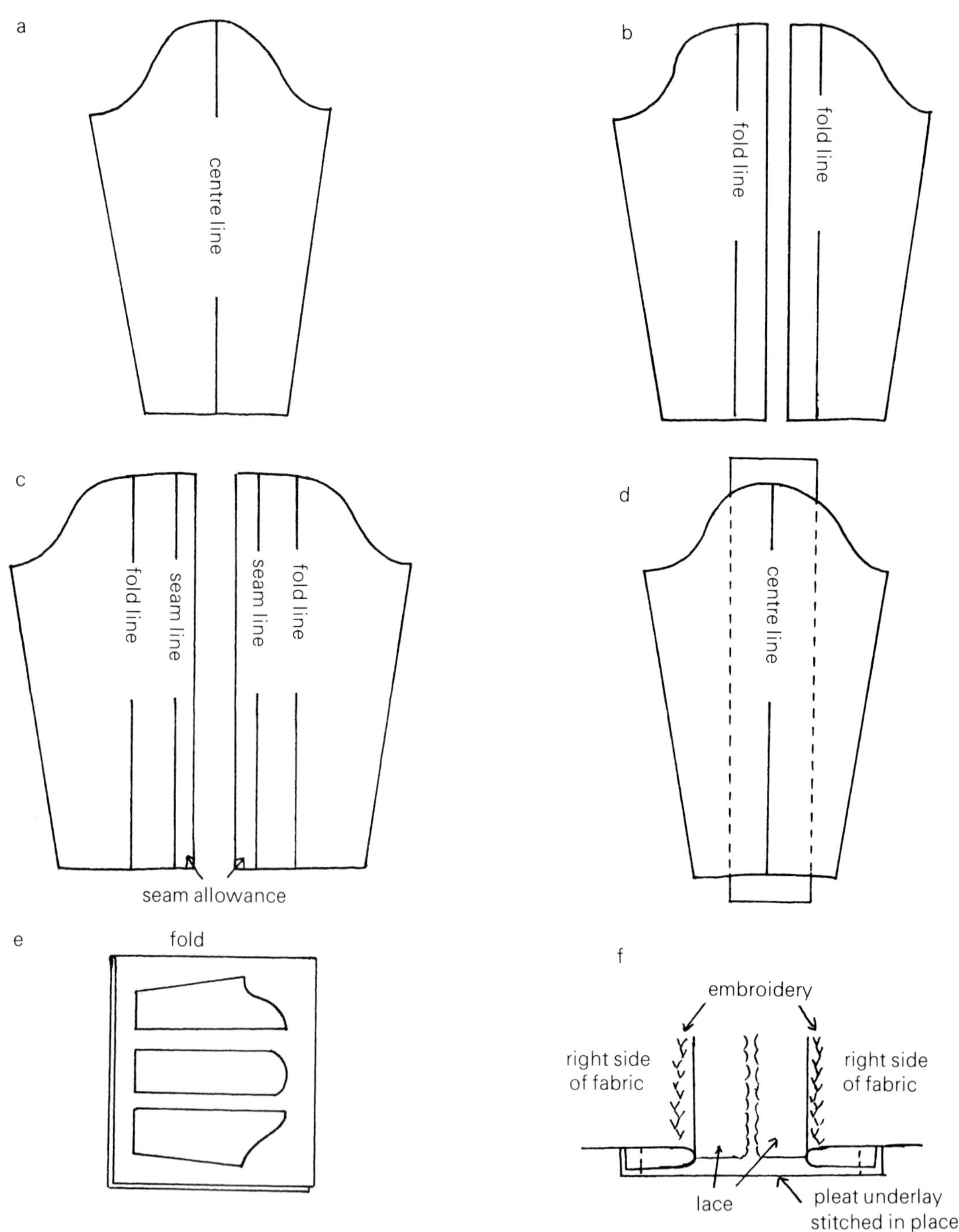

Fig. 100
a–d Adapting the sleeve
pattern
e Pattern layout for cutting
f Layers of finished pleat

Making up the blouse   Make the blouse up in the usual way. On the original I also worked feather stitch (to match that on the sleeve) along the edges of the yoke, down the front edge and round the collar in place of machine-top stitching. The concealed buttonhole band is also attached with a line of feather stitch worked through all layers.

Alternatives   1) The lace could be made to match the blouse and the pleat underlay could be in fabric of a contrasting colour.
2) A strip of lace could be applied round the cuffs. By omitting the footside pinholes and working a picot edge along both sides, a strip suitable for this purpose can be made; this is illustrated on page 86 of *Mounting and Using Lace*, where a frill edged with the same lace has been added to a cuff.
3) The same idea could be adapted for use on a skirt, using a coarser lace. The lace could disappear into either the waistband or into a yoke. In this case the lace would need to be started neatly and attractively for the hem edge of the skirt because the ends could not be concealed. Fig. 101 illustrates three suggestions.
4) The jabot on page 70 could be made in fabric and thread to match the lace on this blouse, as illustrated in Fig. 96.

Fig. 101 Ideas for skirts with lace-edged pleats

Blouse with square neckline & sleeve ruffles

The lace and the neckline of the blouse both need careful planning before starting so that they will fit together accurately and the lace will have complete pattern repeats on each side, remembering that the cloth stitch and half stitch shapes alternate. The footside of the outer edging should be longer than that of the inner edging so that on the finished blouse there will be a strip of fabric visible between them; on the original, this was 2.5 cm (1 inch) wide. Fig. 104c indicates the number of repeats used on the original blouse.

Choose a short-sleeved style with a square neckline (or adapt your own). If there is no front or back fastening, the lace can be made as a closed border; the neckline will be able to be pulled over the head. If required, a zip can be inserted into the side seam of the blouse. Each sleeve is finished with a circular ruffle trimmed with a circular piece of lace.

Do *not* cut out the neckline until the lace has been made.

The blouse illustrated in Fig. 102 and the lace illustrated in Fig. 103 were made by June Jackson, using lace designed by the author.

Materials Tanne No. 30 –
Pricking in Fig. 104a – edging with outer corner – 19 pairs
Pricking in Fig. 104b – edging with inner corner – 19 pairs
Pricking in Fig. 104d – $\frac{1}{4}$ circle – 19 pairs
Suitable material and pattern for blouse

The lace For the neckline, arrange to have the join in the lace just to the back of the shoulder seam, where it will be least conspicuous.

Start with a cloth stitch section as indicated in Figs 105a and b. The working is quite straightforward, Fig. 105c indicating by dashes the twisting of passives and weavers in the scallop. Remember on half-stitch sections to change the weavers (see note 2 on page 11). Take particular care when working the corners to work the correct sections in cloth stitch or half stitch as shown in Figs 103 and 105. Note that on the circular pricking there are more pinholes on each scallop, but they are worked in a similar way. To finish off, the three edge pairs may be darned into the fabric or hem, and the remainder into the cloth-stitch trail.

Fig. 102 Blouse with square neckline and sleeve ruffles

Fig. 103 Detail of lace on blouse illustrated in Fig. 102

116

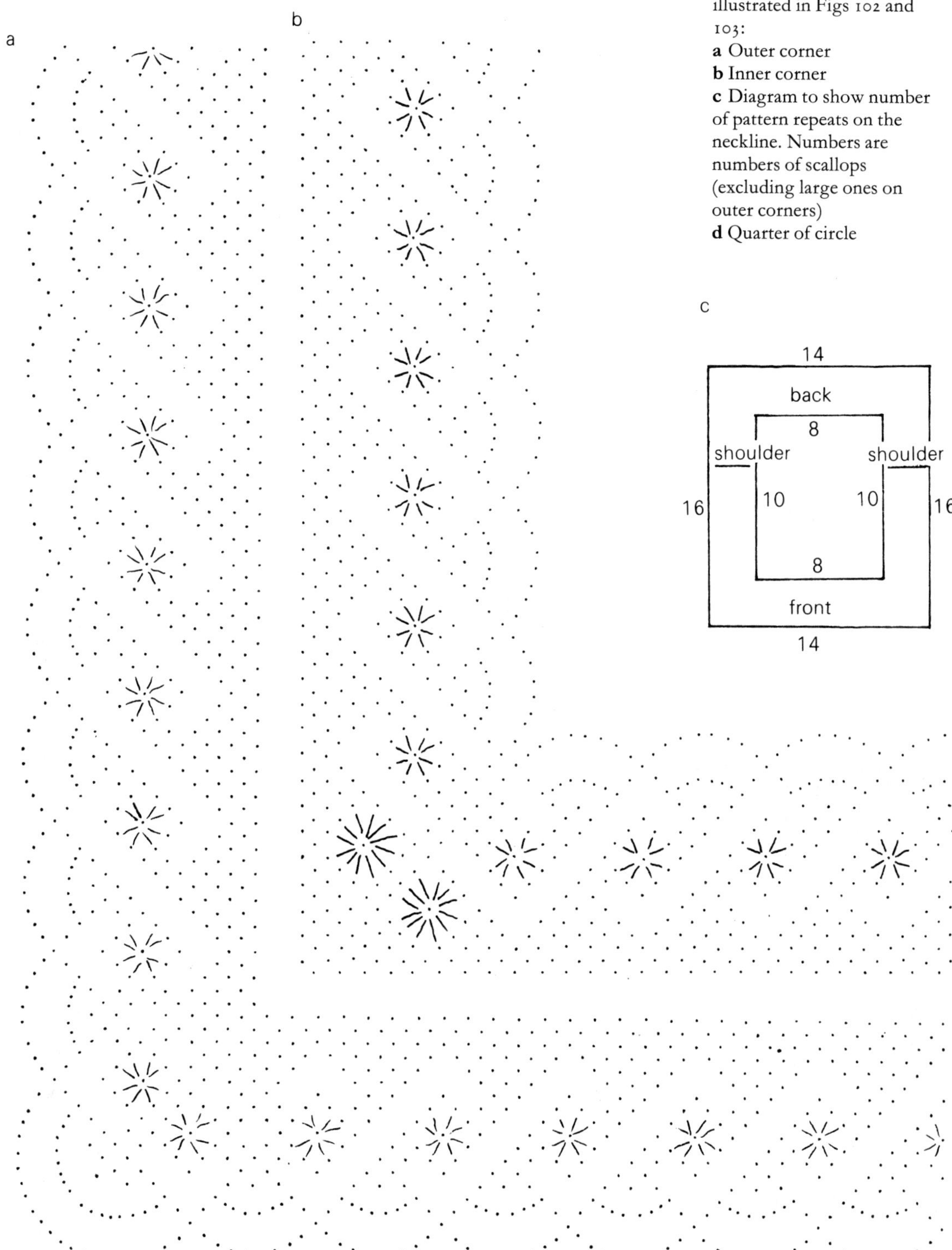

Fig. 104 Prickings for lace illustrated in Figs 102 and 103:
a Outer corner
b Inner corner
c Diagram to show number of pattern repeats on the neckline. Numbers are numbers of scallops (excluding large ones on outer corners)
d Quarter of circle

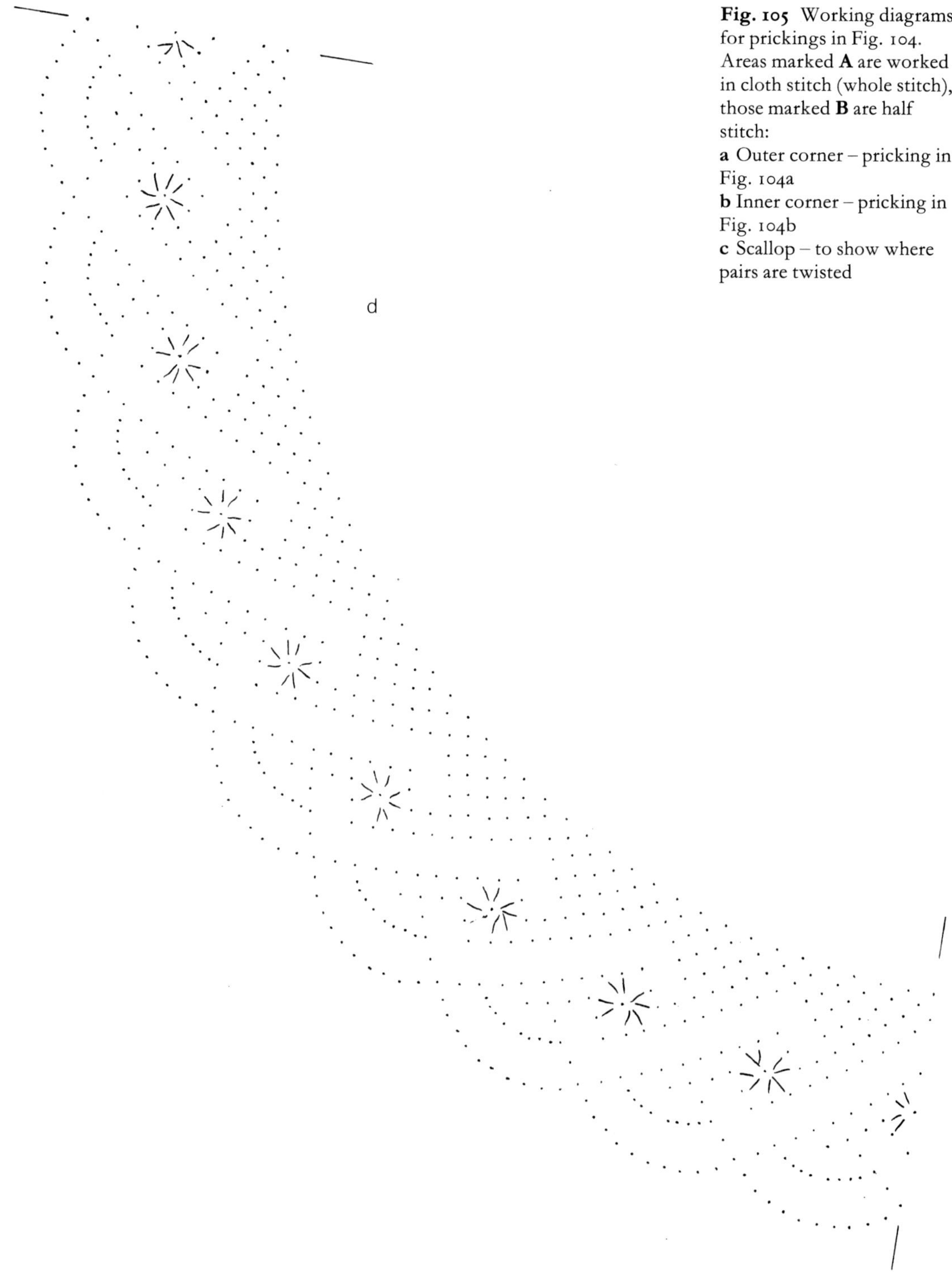

Fig. 105 Working diagrams for prickings in Fig. 104. Areas marked **A** are worked in cloth stitch (whole stitch), those marked **B** are half stitch:
a Outer corner – pricking in Fig. 104a
b Inner corner – pricking in Fig. 104b
c Scallop – to show where pairs are twisted

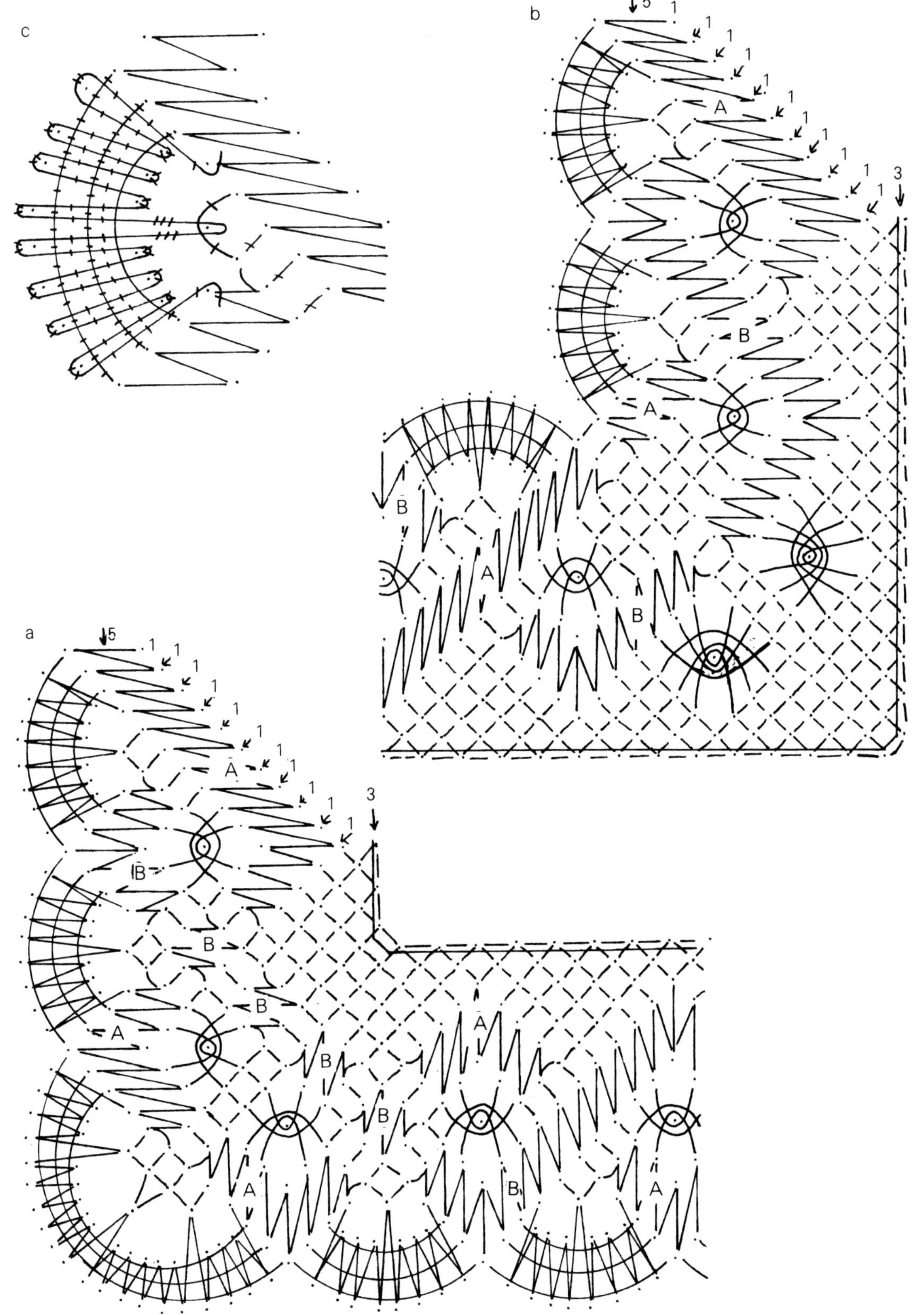

c
b
↓5 1 1 1 1
1 1
A
1 1
1 3
B
A
B
A
B
a
↓5 1 1 1
1 1
A
1 1
1 3
B
B
A
A
B
B
A
B
A
↓5
A

To adapt the pattern, mark the position of the footside edge of the inner lace edging, add seam allowances and cut out the new neckline. Make patterns for back and front facings to fit the neckline. Stitch the shoulder seams in both blouse and facing, press flat and then pin the facing to the neckline with the right side of the facing and the wrong side of the blouse together. Stitch round the neckline, layer and clip the seams and turn the facing out to the right side of the blouse. Now turn under the raw edges on the outer edge of the facing, adjusting the width so that the finished width will be the same as the distance between the footside edges of the two pieces of lace – 2.5 cm (1 inch) on the original. When the facing has been top-stitched along this folded edge and the other edge, it will appear as a band between the two pieces of lace, which can be stitched into place when the facing has been completed. If you prefer, the facing could be used on the inside of the neckline in the usual way.

To make the paper pattern for the sleeve ruffle, draw a circle the same diameter as the footside edge of the completed lace circle, making sure that the centre point will be visible later. Measure the width of the sleeve pattern (without seams) at the bottom, where the ruffle will be attached; this will be the circumference of the smaller circle. Using the formula:

$$\frac{\text{Circumference}}{6.28} = \text{Radius}$$

work out the radius of this circle and draw it inside the first one, making its centre point about 2.5 cm (1 inch) from that of the larger circle. This is an actual size pattern, so add seam allowances before cutting out. Note that it is better not to cut out the centre hole until after the lace has been attached, so that the bias areas are not stretched out of shape.

To make up the ruffle, stitch the lace into place using three-sided stitch for strength. If the fabric is suitable, avoid using a hem or bias binding to finish the fabric, because a bulky hem would not drape well. Then seam the inner edge of the fabric circle and the lower edge of the sleeve together, clipping the seam allowances on the circle so that it will lie flat and with the narrowest part of the ruffle at the front of the sleeve. Arrange for the join in the lace to be just to the back of the sleeve side seam, where it will be least conspicuous.

1) This neckline and sleeve ruffle could also be used for a wedding dress.
2) The same idea for a ruffle could be used with other prickings for circular lace if they are of a suitable size, and a smaller circular pricking could be used in this way on a full-length sleeve.
3) These three prickings can be combined in a variety of ways – see Figs 36 and 106 for some suggestions. The pricking illustrated in Fig. 104d and a straight strip of the pricking could be used together to make an apron edging; see Fig. 76. Also, consider combining them with embroidery.

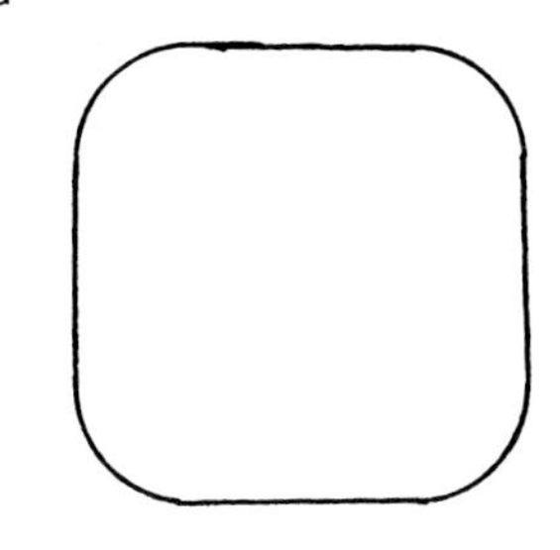

Fig. 106 Suggestions for combining prickings in Fig. 104:
a Quarter circle and straight edging
b Inner and outer corners
c Semicircles and inner corners
d Suggestion for using shapes in **b** and **c**, over a plain contrasting tablecloth. Adjust the length of straight sections of the pricking to suit

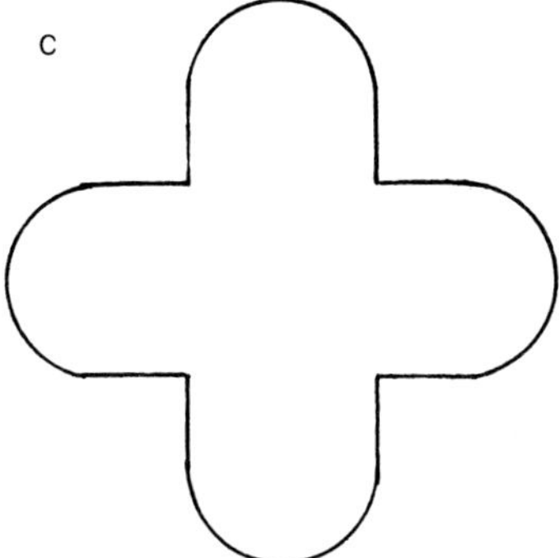

Collar with Honiton-type edging

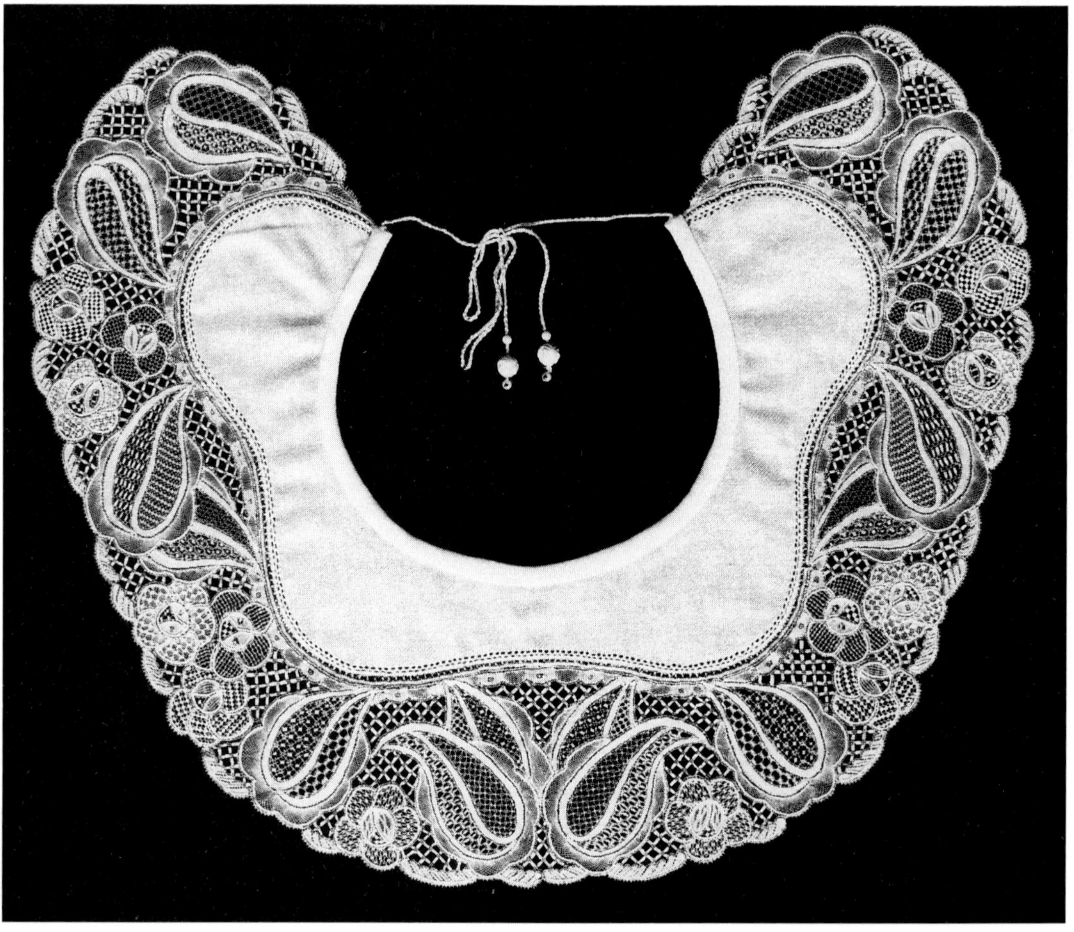

Fig. 107 Collar with Honiton-type edging

This collar is illustrated in Fig. 107 and a detail in Fig. 108; further illustrations also appear on pages 21, 29 and 84 of *Mounting and Using Lace*, showing other areas in detail and the finished article being worn. The lace involves both raised and rolled work and a variety of fillings; if it appears too ambitious, make one or two motifs which can be used for any of the purposes suggested below – if successful, this may encourage you to proceed further!

Adaptations 1) Any one of the Paisley-type motifs could be used in a variety of ways – for example:

a) Mounted in a frame; one from the pricking in Fig. 109a is illustrated used in this way on page 13 of *Mounting and Using Lace*

b) In an oval paperweight, choosing the motif you prefer as they vary in size and shape

c) Several could be used down the sleeves of a blouse – see page 94

d) One could be used on a patch pocket, for example on a skirt or dress

2) Any of the complete flower motifs from the prickings in Figs 110a and 113a could be used as follows:

a) One could be framed

b) On a serviette ring (see page 23)
c) Several could be used on a bridal head-dress (see page 65)

Materials
Wigley No. 180 cotton
Brilliante d'Alsace No. 30 as a coarse thread
Fabric to match – for the original I used a wool/cotton mixture
because it was the only fabric that exactly matched the lace

The lace
I have assumed a working knowledge of Honiton lace; all the techniques and fillings are fully described in *The Technique of Honiton Lace* and *Honiton Lace Patterns*, both by Elsie Luxton, *A Manual of Hand-Made Bobbin Lace Work* by Margaret Maidment or *The Book of Bobbin Lace Stitches* by Bridget Cook and Geraldine Stott. The fillings I used are given merely as a guide – choose your own if you prefer, noting that all the fillings must be pricked in from a grid. By working in the following order the length of time that large pieces of lace are on the pillow is kept to a minimum.

Note that to obtain prickings 110b, 111b, 112b, 113b and 114b you will need to place a piece of paper between the pricking card and the copy of the pricking when preparing the prickings in figs 110a, 111a, 112a, 113a and 114a; turn this paper over and use it to prick from the opposite side to obtain a mirror image.

On the working diagrams, a heavy line indicates a rib or roll; I used seven pairs for all of these. Where there are adjacent pinholes on motifs, the motifs are joined by sewings as you work past the pinhole already worked. This is a rule to be observed throughout.

Diamond filling has been used as a ground for this collar. When used in this way it can be pricked at the same angle throughout the piece or can be arranged so that its angle to the footside is maintained, as was done on the original. The outer edge of the lace is finished with a purl edge; whilst this can be worked during the construction of the lace, I found it easier to sew the purls onto the completed lace, section by section, before removing it from the pillow.

Refer to figs 109a and 109c, which are the pricking and working diagram for the centre back. Begin with the complete Paisley motif on the right-hand side as follows:

Begin the cloth stitch braid at 1. Work round following the arrows and sew out at 2, bunching the threads and cutting them off. Now sew in pairs at 3 and work a cloth stitch braid to 4, where the pairs are sewn out, bunched and cut off.

Sew in pairs at 5 for a rib (ten stick), and work round to 6 where the runners and edge pairs are sewn in and used to bunch the remaining pairs. All these pairs are then used to fill the half stitch section, adding extra pairs if necessary and finishing at 5 where the threads are sewn, bunched and cut off.

Work the fillings, Jubilee in space **B** and Toad-in-the-Hole with Wide Leadworks in space **C**.

Next work the complete motif on the left-hand side as a mirror

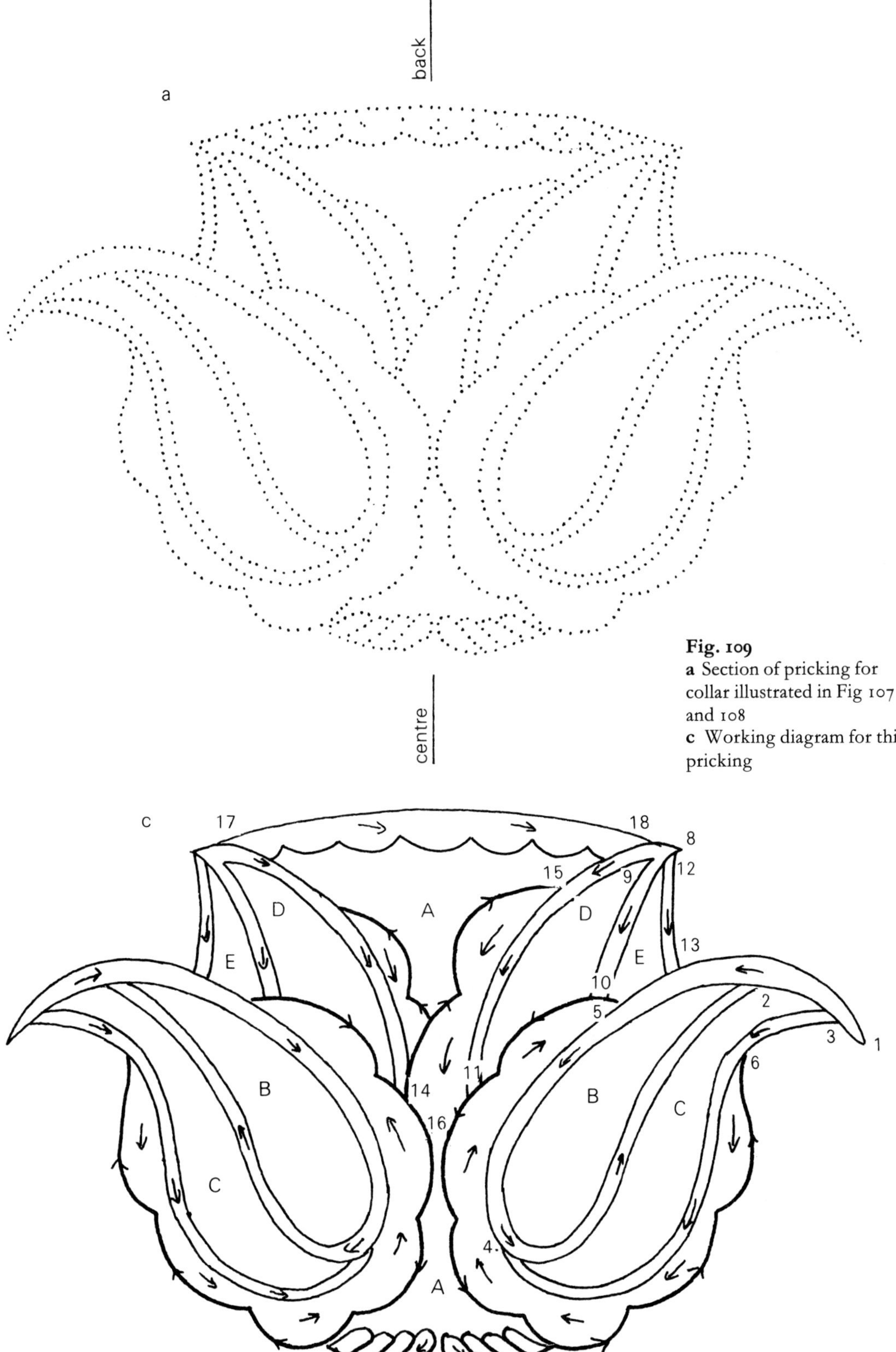

Fig. 109
a Section of pricking for collar illustrated in Fig 107 and 108
c Working diagram for this pricking

image of the motif just completed, remembering to join them together by sewings as mentioned above.

Sew in pairs at 7 to work the tap leaf on the right, and then work the tap leaf on the left as a mirror image.

Now start the part motif on the right by beginning a cloth stitch braid at 8. Divide this braid into two at 9 and continue these braids down to 10 and 11 respectively, where they are sewn out, bunched and cut off. For the remaining short cloth stitch braid, sew in at 12 and finish off at 13.

Sew in pairs for a rib at 14 and work round to 15, where the rib is attached to the braid; the pairs are then used to fill the half stitch section, adding pairs as necessary and finishing at 16.

The fillings for this motif are Four-Pin with Leadworks in space **D**, and Whole Stitch Block Variation in space **E**.

The remaining motif is worked in a similar way.

For the braid across the top, sew in at 17 and finish off at 18, working alternate sections in cloth stitch with a four-pin bud and half stitch. Complete this pricking by working Diamond filling in the spaces marked **A**. Remove the lace and pricking from the pillow.

Now refer to Figs 110a and 110c. Pin the lace already made onto this pricking where indicated, making sure that the lace is face down.

Start the Paisley motif at the point (at 1) and work the central cloth stitch braid. Follow the arrows round to the right-hand side and back up to the top, where this braid crosses the existing braid. Carry on down the left-hand side to 2, where the threads are sewn, bunched and cut off.

Sew in pairs for a rib at 3 and work round to 4, where the rib is attached to the braid. Now fill the half stitch section back to 3, where the threads are sewn, bunched and cut off.

Work the fillings, Blossom Variation in space **B** and Whole Stitch Block in space **C** (both described in *Honiton Lace Patterns*, by Elsie Luxton).

Next work the flower. Start with a rib at 5 and work round the central circle; attach it to the starting point and then continue the rib up to 6. Attach the rib to the circle and then use these pairs (adding extra ones where necessary) to fill the leaf shape back to 5. This shape is filled with cloth stitch decorated with four twisted veins.

Reduce to seven pairs by the time pin 5 is reached, and then use these pairs to roll up to 7. Rib on to 8, where it is attached to the circle. The leaf shape is then filled in the same way back to pin 5, again reducing to seven pairs by the time that pin is reached. Do *not* cut these threads off.

To outline the petals, sew in seven pairs for a rib at 9 and use these to work round the complete petal to 10, where the rib is attached to the circle. Now roll these pairs up to 11 and then rib round to 12, where they are sewn in, bunched and cut off.

Now return to the pairs left at 5, and use them to rib round to 13 where they are sewn, bunched and cut off.

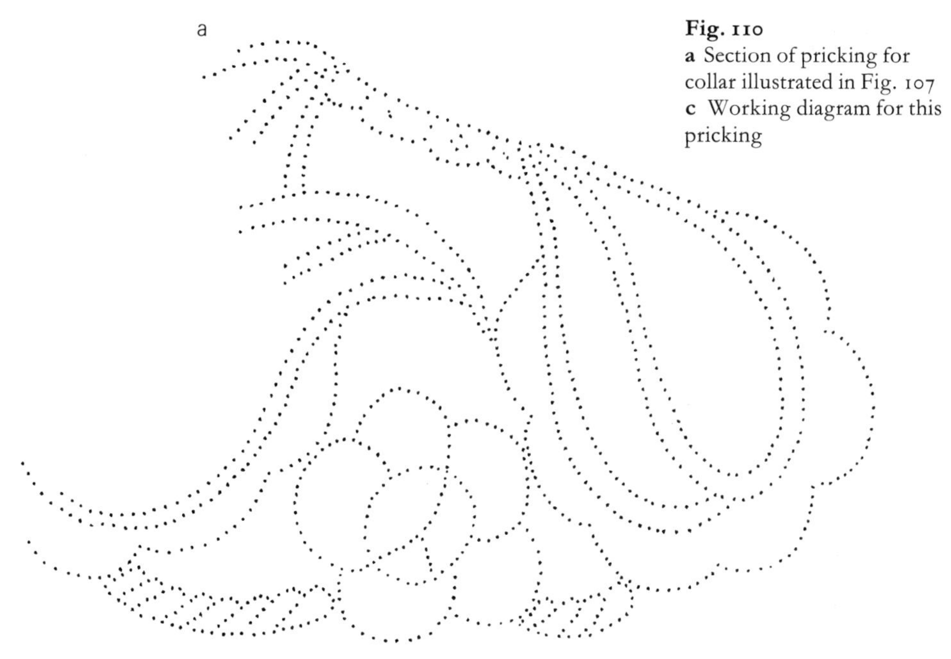
a

Fig. 110
a Section of pricking for
collar illustrated in Fig. 107
c Working diagram for this
pricking

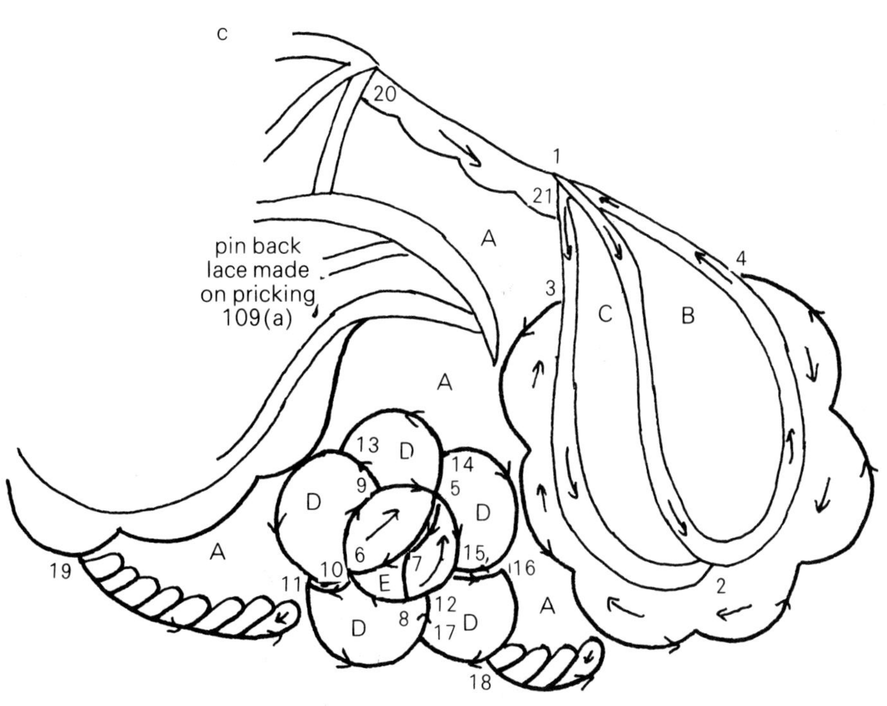
c
20
1
21
A
pin back
lace made
on pricking
109(a)
3
A
C
B
4
A
13 D
14
9
5
D
D
A
10
6
7
15
16
11
E
19
12
D 8 17 D
A
2
18

Sew in pairs at 14 and rib round to 15, where the rib is attached to the circle. Use the pairs to roll up to 16 and rib to 17, where they are sewn out, bunched and cut off.

Complete the flower by working Cutwork and Pinhole filling in the spaces marked **D**, and No Pin in space **E**. For all the flowers in this collar, start working the filling from the outer edge of the petals towards the centre, where the threads can be sewn out neatly.

Work the two tap leaves, sewing in pairs at 18 and 19 respectively, then work the short length of braid at the top from 20 to 21. Complete this section of the lace by working Diamond filling into all the spaces labelled **A**.

Remove the lace and pricking from the pillow and now work pricking 110b, pinning the lace back onto this pricking in the correct position. Work this pricking as a mirror image of 110a, remove the completed piece of lace and lay it to one side.

For the front section of the collar, refer to Figs 111a and 111c. Begin the cloth stitch braid for the right-hand motif at 1; continue down the centre, up the right-hand side, cross over the previously worked braid and down the left-hand side to 2, where the pairs are sewn out, bunched and cut off.

Sew in the pairs for the rib at 3, work round to 4, attach to the braid and fill with half stitch back to 3, where the threads are sewn, bunched and cut off.

Work the left-hand motif in a similar way, starting at 5 and working down the centre. Follow the arrows, crossing the braid over the existing one, right round to 6 where the pairs are sewn, bunched and cut off.

The rib is worked from 7 round to 8, and then filled back with half stitch to 7, where the pairs are sewn, bunched and cut off.

Work the fillings in spaces as follows – Toad-in-the-Hole in **B**, Four-Pin in **C**, Whole Stitch Block (as described in Margaret Maidment's book) in **D** and Blossom (as described in Elsie Luxton's books) in **E**.

Now work the top tap leaf, starting it at 9, and the next tap leaf is started at 10 by sewing pairs into the first one. The remaining two tap leaves are worked in a similar way, starting at 11 and 12 respectively.

The top braid is started at 13 and finished at 14. Complete this section by working Diamond filling into all the spaces marked **A**. Remove the lace and pricking from the pillow and set aside the lace.

The next section to be worked is that which includes one complete and one part Paisley motif, and lies across the shoulders. Refer to Figs 112a and 112c and start the complete motif at 1, working the cloth stitch braid down the centre. Following the arrows, cross the braid over the existing one at the top, and finish at 2.

Now work a rib starting at 3 and continuing to 4, where it is attached to the braid before filling with half stitch back to 3 where the threads are sewn, bunched and cut off. Work Italian filling in

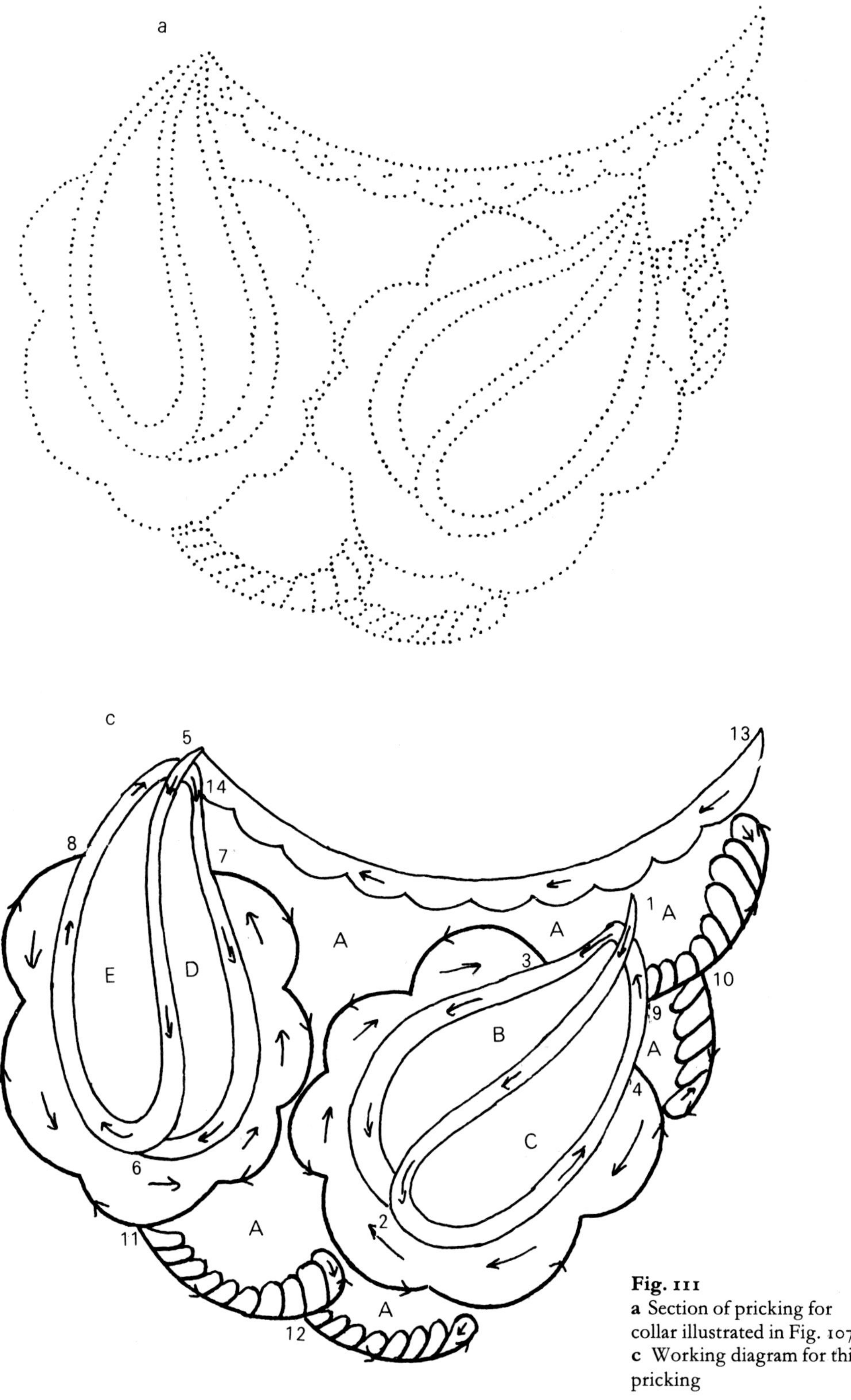

Fig. III
a Section of pricking for collar illustrated in Fig. 107
c Working diagram for this pricking

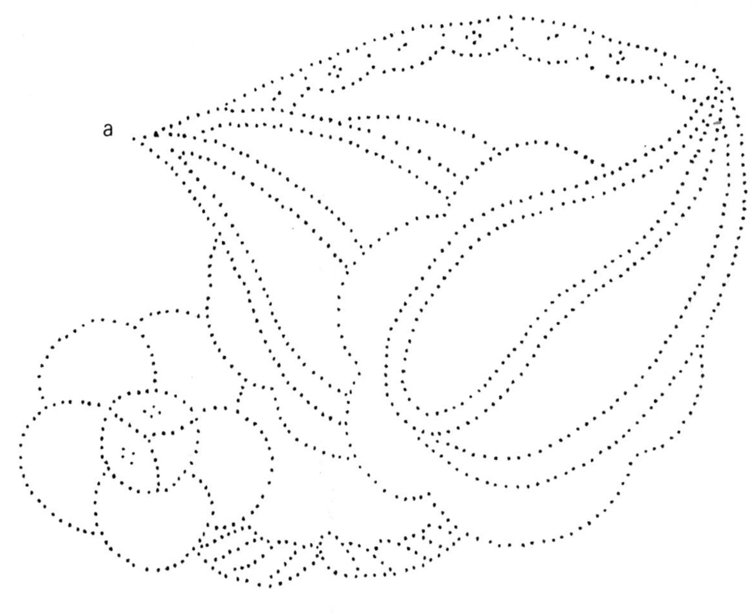

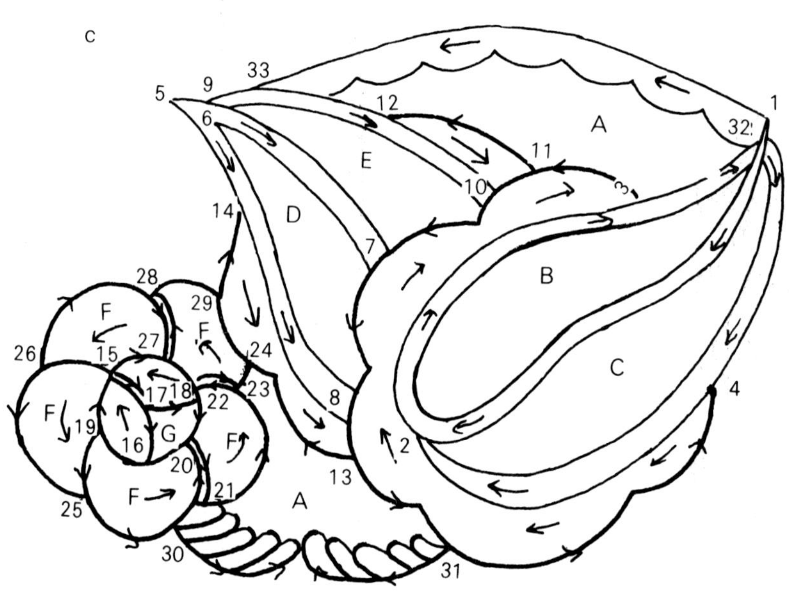

Fig. 112
a Section of pricking for
collar illustrated in Fig. 107
c Working diagram for this
pricking

space **B** and Straight Pin in space **C**.

The incomplete motif is started at 5 with a braid which divides at 6, the two sections ending at 7 and 8 respectively. The remaining cloth stitch section starts at 9 and ends at 10.

Sew in pairs for a rib at 11 and work to 12, then fill back with half stitch. Note that when these pairs are sewn out along the line between 10 and 11, they are not bunched. Next sew in pairs at 13, rib to 14 and then fill back to 13 with half stitch. Work the fillings – Toad-in-the Hole Variation in space **D** and Devonshire Honeycomb (described in *The Book of Bobbin Lace Stitches*, by Bridget Cook and Geraldine Stott) in space **E**.

The flower is worked next. Start with a rib at 15 and work round the circle back to this pin, where the rib is attached. Continue the rib up to 16 and then fill back to 15, working in cloth stitch with a four pin bud. From 15, roll up to 17 and rib on to 18. Fill this shape back to 15 in the same way. Leave the threads here but do *not* cut them off.

At 19, sew in pairs for a rib and work round the complete petal to 20, attach the rib to the circle at 20, then roll up to 21 and rib round to 22. From here, roll up to 23 and then rib to 24, where the threads are sewn out, bunched and cut off.

Return to the threads left at 15 and rib round to 25, where the threads are sewn out, bunched and cut off. To complete the outline of the petals, sew in pairs at 26, rib to 27, attach to the circle and then roll to 28 and rib to 29, where it is sewn out and the threads bunched and cut off. Work No Pin filling in **G** and Brick filling in the spaces marked **F**, working from the outer edges towards the centre. Complete the petals by working half stitch over the filling, working round the flower in the direction of the arrows in spaces **F**.

Work the two tap leaves, starting at 30 and 31 respectively, and the top braid from 32 to 33. Finally, fill the spaces marked **A** with Diamond filling.

Remove the lace from the pillow. The next section to be worked will join this section and the front section previously worked on pricking 111a. Refer to Figs 113a and 113c; place the pricking on the pillow and then pin back the last section of lace made (from pricking 112a) as indicated, and then pin on the front section (from pricking 111a) at the opposite end, also as indicated.

Begin with the top flower by starting a rib at 1 and work round the circle, joining the rib into the starting pinhole. Now use these pairs to rib up to 2 and then fill the leaf back to 1. On this flower, the leaf shapes are filled with cloth stitch and a twisted vein. From pin 1, roll to 3 and then rib to 4. Now fill back to 1 as before. Use these pairs to rib round the complete petal to 5, attach to the circle, roll to 6 and then rib to 7. Continue round each petal in turn, rolling and ribbing as necessary until the rib reaches 9, where it is sewn out and the threads bunched and cut off.

The remaining two flower centres and petal outlines are worked in the same way, following the arrows for the direction of work. The centre of the right-hand flower is filled with half stitch and that of

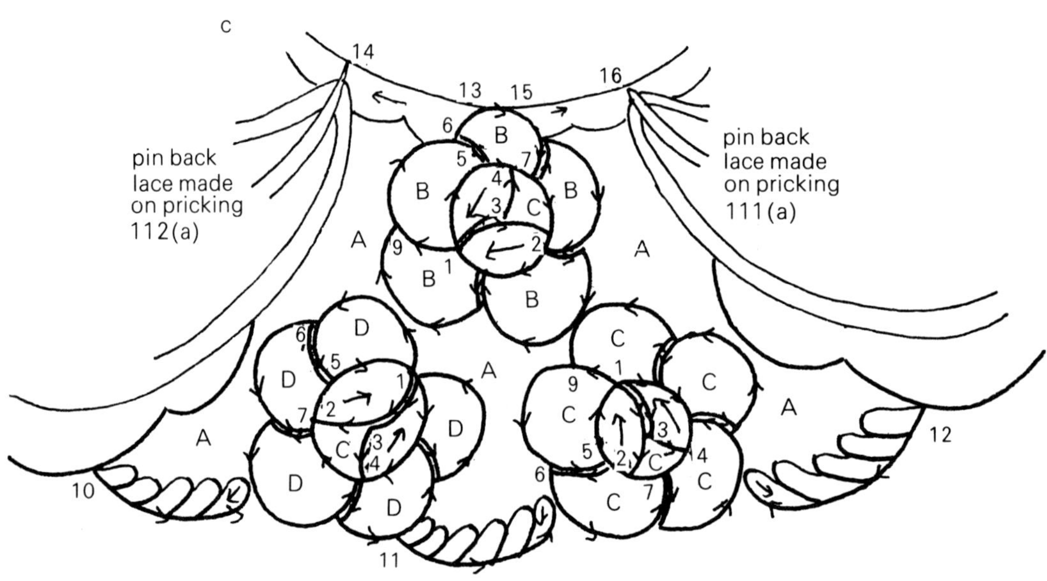

Fig. 113
a Section of pricking for
collar illustrated in Fig. 107
c Working diagram for this
pricking

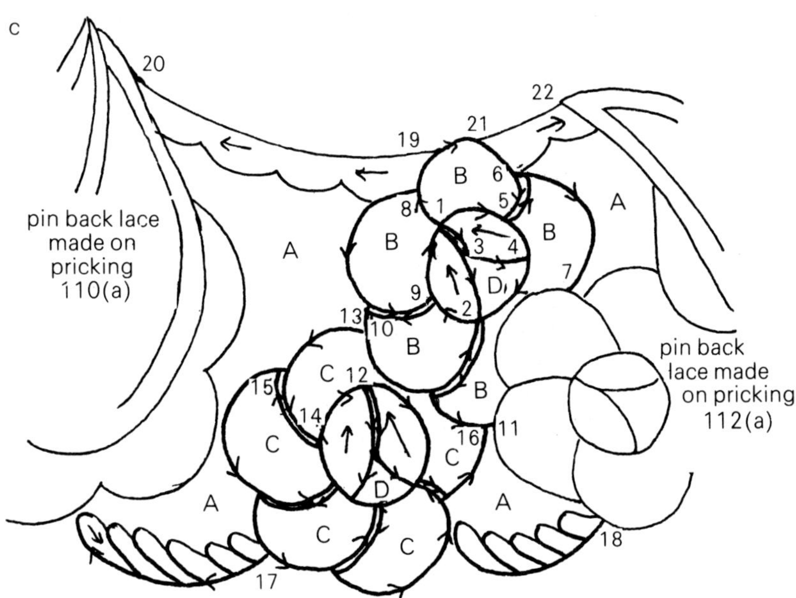

Fig. 114
a Section of pricking for
collar illustrated in Fig. 107
c Working diagram for this
pricking

the left-hand one with divided cloth stitch connected by leadworks.

The fillings for the flowers are Pin-and-a-Stitch in **B**, No Pin in **C** and Devonshire Cutwork with half stitch worked over it in **D**.

The three tap leaves begin at 10, 11 and 12 respectively, and two short lengths of braid are worked at the top from 13 to 14 and from 15 to 16.

Complete this section by working Diamond filling in the spaces marked **A** and then remove the lace and pricking from the pillow.

The two sections of lace which are complete are now joined by working pricking 114a. Refer to working diagram 114c and pin back both pieces of lace as indicated.

Begin with the top flower. Starting at 1, work a rib round the centre ring, attach to the starting pin and then rib up to 2. Fill back to 1 in cloth stitch with a snatch pin hole and leadwork in the centre. Roll up to 3, rib to 4 and fill back to 1. From 1, rib round to 5, roll to 6 and rib round to 7 where the threads are sewn, bunched and cut off.

Sew in pairs at 8 to rib to 9, and roll back to 10. Continue working the remaining petals in the same way, sewing out, bunching and cutting off the threads at 11.

For the left-hand flower, start at 12 and work the centre in the usual way, filling the leaf shapes with whole stitch and twisting the runners three times each time they make a stitch. When both shapes have been filled, sew out and cut off the threads.

To outline the petals, sew in at 13, rib round to 14 and then roll back to 15. Continue round the petal in this way to 16, where the threads are sewn, bunched and cut off.

Work the fillings in the flowers – Pin and a Chain in **B**, Swing and a Stitch in **C** and No Pin in **D**.

Work the two tap leaves starting at 17 and 18 respectively, then work the two sections of braid at the top, working in the direction indicated by the arrows. Finally, work Diamond filling into all the spaces marked **A** before removing the lace from the pillow.

Complete the lace by working prickings 111b, 112b, 113b and 114b in the same order, to match.

To prepare the pricking for the separate cucumber foot braid, fold a large piece of paper in half and place Fig. 115 on top of it with the *fold* line on the fold in the paper. Then prick the pinholes through all the layers. Remove Fig. 115, open out the folded paper and use this to make the pricking.

Work the braid, putting in thread markers at the arrows; these will help in positioning the lace, each arrow being in line with a point where a Paisley motif cuts the braid edge of the collar.

Fig. 115 gives the pattern for the fabric part of the collar; there are no seam allowances. To complete the collar, attach the braid to the fabric using three-sided stitch; finish the neck edge with a matching bias strip (as described on page 93) and overcast the lace into place on the braid. The collar may be fastened with ties or hook and eye, or the bias-bound edge can be tacked inside the neckline of the dress.

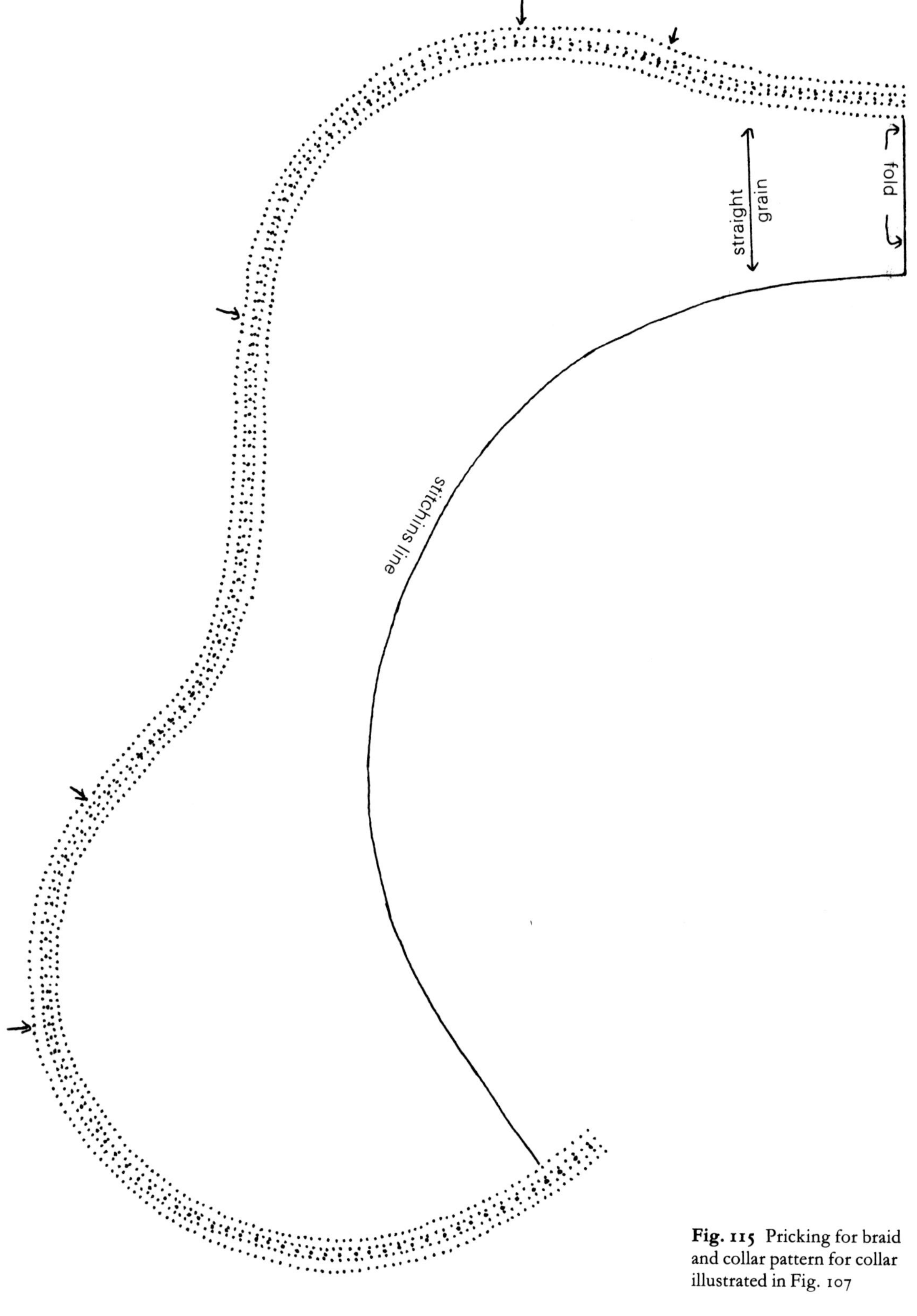

Fig. 115 Pricking for braid and collar pattern for collar illustrated in Fig. 107

Further reading

A wide range of books on lacemaking and embroidery is available;
the following are a few suggestions.

Ambuter, Carolyn, *The Open Canvas*, Penguin
Cave, Oenone, *Linen Cut Work*, Vista, republished by Dover
Cook, Bridget & Stott, Geraldine, *The Book of Bobbin Lace Stitches*,
    Batsford
Fishburn, Angela, *Lampshades – Technique and Design*, Batsford
Luxton, Elsie, *Honiton Lace Patterns*, Batsford
Luxton, Elsie, *The Technique of Honiton Lace*, Batsford
Maidment, Margaret, *A Manual of Hand-Made Bobbin Lace Work*,
    Pitman, republished by Batsford
McNeill, Moyra, *Pulled Thread*, Bell & Hyman
Nottingham, Pamela, *The Technique of Bobbin Lace*, Batsford
Mary Thomas' Dictionary of Embroidery Stitches, Hodder & Stoughton
Mary Thomas' Embroidery Book, Hodder & Stoughton
Withers, Jean, *Mounting and Using Lace*, Dryad Press
Anchor Manual of Needlework, Batsford

Suppliers

Chrisken Bobbins
26 Cedar Drive
Kingsclere
Newbury
Berks RG15 8TD

*(Inlaid bobbins and pen pots
for mounting lace – mail order
service)*

Framecraft Miniatures Ltd
148/150 High Street
Aston
Birmingham

*(Range of gilt and silver ware
suitable for mounting – mail
order service)*

Stuart Johnson Lace Bobbins
The Stables
The Holloway
Market Place
Warwick

*(Bobbins and pillows – mail
order service)*

Margaret & Malcolm Thorpe
36 Twyford Road
Ward End
Birmingham B8 2NJ

*(Laminated bobbins – mail
order service)*

Joan Kelly
39 Copeland Avenue
Tittensor
Stoke-on-Trent
Staffs ST12 9JA

*(Wide range of lace threads
and general lace supplies,
including coloured
handkerchiefs – mail order
service)*

Ribbon Designs
42 Lake View
Edgware
Mddx HA8 7RU

*(Embroidery ribbons – mail
order service)*

Janet Smith (Lace Supplies)
77 Falmouth Avenue
Weeping Cross
Stafford ST17 0JG

*(General supplies, evenweave
cottons including some colours
and matching lace threads –
mail order service)*

Alby Lace Centre
Cromer Road
Alby
Norwich
Norfolk

Frank Herring & Sons
27 High West Street
Dorchester
DT1 1UP

Honiton Lace Shop
44 High Street
Honiton
Devon

D J Hornsby
149 High Street
Burton Latimer
Kettering
Northants

Capt J R Howell
19 Summerwood Lane
Halsall
Nr Ormskirk
Lancs L39 8RG

Sebalace
Waterloo Mill
Howden Road
Silsden
West Yorks
BD20 0HA

George White
Delaheys Cottage
Thistle Hill
Knaresborough
North Yorks

C & D Springett
29 Hillmorton Road
Rugby
Warwicks CV22 5BE

A Sells
49 Pedley Lane
Clifton
Shefford
Beds

Enid Taylor
Valley House Craft Studio
Ruston
Scarborough
North Yorks YO13 9QE

Newham Lace Equipment
11 Dorchester Close
Basingstoke
Hants

English Lace School
Honiton Court
Rockbeare
Nr Exeter
Devon

T Brown
Woodside
Greenlands Lane
Prestwood
Great Missenden
Bucks

Mace and Nairn
89 Crane Street
Salisbury
Wilts

The Lace Guild
The Hollies
53 Audnam
Stourbridge
West Midlands

D H Shaw
47 Zamor Crescent
Thurscroft
Rotherham
South Yorks

Shireburn Lace
Finkle Court
Finkle
Sherburn in Elmet
North Yorks

B Phillips
Pantglas
Cellan
Lampeter
Dyfed

Lichfield Needlework Centre
5 St John Street
Lichfield
Staffordshire
WS13 6NU

Dryad Press lace books

Gillian Dye, *Beginning Bobbin Lace*.
Jennifer Fisher, *Braid Lace for Today*.
Edna Sutton, *Bruges Flower Lace*.
Neilli O'Cleirigh, *Carrickmacross Lace*.
Ros Hills, *Colour and Texture in Needlelace*.
Levá-Skrovánová/Stan Skoumal, *Contemporary Bohemian Lace*.
Valerie Paton, *Creative Lace Patterns*.
Edna Sutton, *Designing for Bruges Flower Lace*.
Alexandra Stillwell, *Drafting Torchon Lace Patterns*.
Raie Clare, *Dryad Book of Bobbin Lace*.
Doreen Holmes, *Flowers in Needlepoint Lace*.
Eithne D'Arcy, *Irish Crochet Lace*.
Eileen O'Connor, *Irish Lace Making*.
C. C. Channer & M. Waller, *Lacemaking Point Ground*.
Valerie Harris, *Lavendon Collection of Bobbin Lace*.
Veronica Rowe, *Limerick Lace*.
Jean Withers, *Mounting and Using Lace*.
Edna Groves, *A New Approach to Embroidered Net*.
Elwyn Kenn, *Point Ground Patterns from Australia*.
Nenia Lovesey, *Punto Tagliato Lace*.
Jennifer Fisher, *Torchon Lace for Today*.
Nenia Lovesey & Catherine Barley, *Venetian Gros Point Lace*.

For further details on all Dryad Press craft titles please write to:

Dryad Press Limited
8 Cavendish Square
London W1M 0AJ

Index